WILBER WINKLE™ HAS A COMPLAINT!

By Wilber Winkle

bancroft
press

BALTIMORE, MD

Published by Bancroft Press, P.O. Box 65360, Baltimore, MD 21209. (410) 358-0658.
www.bancroftpress.com

Library of Congress Catalog Card Number: 96-79742

ISBN 0-9631246-4-1
Printed in the United States of America

Designed by Melinda Russell, Bancroft Press
Cover and interior illustration by Bonnie Matthews, Baltimore, MD
Distributed to the trade by National Book Network, Lanham, MD

To my good friend and special assistant, John Homans.
Without your help, encouragement, and understanding, this book would not have been possible.

CONTENTS

ALL ABOUT ME

Dear Reader:

Like everybody in this world, I've had my share of continuing problems as a consumer. Two examples come immediately to mind: trying to transport ice trays from sink to freezer without making a mess on the kitchen floor, and attempting to get multiple drink refills at fast food restaurants without getting hassled by store managers. You name the adversity and I've suffered through it.

What makes me different, though, is how I've learned to cope. To put it in the language of baseball, after years of strikeouts and double play grounders, I've figured out how to hit. But before I reveal my batting secrets, allow me first to share some of my biggest whiffs, worst at-bats, and missed signals during a remarkable career in personal coping and consumer complaining.

As a high school student in the 1970s, I foolishly thought the best way to handle adversity was with my fists. I idolized Muhammad Ali and was particularly fascinated by his upset victory over George Foreman in Zaire. In that 1974 fight, Ali used his now-famous "rope-a-dope" strategy. When the bell rang for round number one, Ali simply covered up his head and allowed Foreman to relentlessly strike at his elbows and mid-section. After seven bruising rounds, Foreman was all punched out, and Ali, moving to phase two of his strategy, dropped his weary opponent to the canvas. Many boxing pundits called it the greatest fight strategy of all time.

With Ali as my role model, and his rope-a-dope strategy my chief technique and mantra, I began handling the bullies and punks who targeted me for teasing, insults, and other abuse in high school. The results were something less than triumphant. Using gym lockers for back support, I allowed my tormentors to hammer away at my breadbasket, absorbing their blows as best as I could while waiting for them to tire. Unfortunately, they never did, and I never got a chance to mount my Ali-like counter-offensive. After 14 consecutive defeats, a few broken ribs, and several costly locker replacements, I concluded that fighting was not the way to resolve my inter-personal problems.

Still smarting from these high school beatings, I laid low during my college years, but did try several new coping mechanisms, including one I later learned was called verbal fatalism. Whenever difficulties came my way, I didn't get upset. I merely uttered the phrase, "That's life," gazed toward the heavens, and laughed hysterically. This worked well in most situations. But at times, my laughing was considered highly inappropriate, such as when I was robbed at gun point, or the time my dog was hit by a truck.

And there was one other problem: Each time I laughed in the face of an adversity, I eliminated only 98% of my tension, and the "2 percents" remaining continued to mount. In May of 1993, I did some calculations, and realized that verbal fatalism was good for only 50 stressful occurrences. Having subscribed to this philosophy for more than 10 years, I knew I was living on borrowed time.

The next month, while in a very vulnerable state, I finally snapped. Shopping one day, I discovered that the Hershey people had removed, without notice, the two almonds on the top of my favorite candy bar, Fifth Avenue. As usual, I tried to laugh the problem away, but it soon became obvious that my system simply couldn't manage it. Finally, all of the 2 percents I had managed to keep at bay the previous decade came boiling up.

I raced back to the supermarket and confronted the store manager. Tempers began to flare and pretty soon both of us were red-faced and screaming. When he stepped closer to me, I became confused and resorted to one of my old stress-coping mechanisms. I instinctively covered up my face in the Ali "rope-a-dope" position, all but inviting the manager to take some pokes at my mid-section. Unfortunately, he was on to me, and yelled that Foreman was a fool for being suckered into that and he wasn't about to let the same thing happen to him. As I was being dragged out of the store by security, the manager cried out, "Why are you blaming me, anyway? I don't make the candy bar. I only sell it."

After considerable reflection and a long, grueling bail hearing, I realized he was right. Scraping together what little money I had, I took a Greyhound bus to Hershey, Pennsylvania to get some answers directly from the candy mavens. Carrying a sign that read, "Wilber Winkle Has A Complaint," I picketed in front of the Hershey Company headquarters building, trying to create such a furor that the company's brass would have no choice but to hear my consumer grievance face-to-face.

Unfortunately, my picketing failed to gain media attention. And, because the Hershey corporation owns the town (even the street lamps are shaped like Hershey kisses), the city's residents just didn't have the courage to rise up against their oppressive regime and support me. A few days after beginning my protest, I was run out of town — and told in no uncertain terms never to come back.

Still angry upon returning home, I realized that I needed a new outlet to vent my frustrations, a new way to deal with those responsible for bringing such dissatisfaction and unhappiness to my life. Fighting was surely not the answer. It hurt and, even with medical insurance, it was costly. Verbal fatalism had worked — though with some embarrassment — for a full ten years. But it had dramatically failed me in the candy section of my neighborhood supermarket. Traveling the country to gather public support, as I had attempted to do in Hershey, was too time consuming, economically unfeasible, and essentially ineffective.

After a fair amount of soul-searching, and several long, wrenching, deeply philosophical discussions with my mailman, I decided that writing letters might be the answer. It would relieve my stress, plus provide a way to communicate my complaints to the wrongdoers of the business and political worlds. And it worked. After my first letter to Hershey, my blood pressure dropped substantially, and I felt a lot better— physically and emotionally. And my letters helped other people less equipped than I in the art of consumer defense.

Spurred on by this successful correspondence, I became quite busy communicating with the chieftains of American business. I worried on paper about a wide variety of consumer issues, and especially the fine points of packaging and marketing. Letter-writing produced almost instant results.

Numerous corporate representatives assured me that my complaints and suggestions would be referred to the "appropriate personnel" for action. And while I've yet to hear from the "appropriate personnel" in every case, I understand that these things take time. Within the next three years, I expect my letters to produce changes that'll benefit millions.

Among other things, the following will have been produced because of my unrelenting quibbles:

1. A crackdown on waitresses who refill coffee mugs when we still have coffee left, thereby destroying our delicate, complicated sugar-cream-coffee balances.

2. The total elimination of "give a penny, take a penny" jars that have gained such wild popularity in convenience stores throughout the nation.

3. The return of release mechanisms on all ice cube trays (they mysteriously disappeared years ago).

4. The end of cupcake wrappers as we know them — the ones that always stick to the icing.

5. And the removal of the menacing devil on "Underwood Deviled Ham" cans.

Who couldn't be proud of such immense progress?!

Very truly yours,

Wilber Winkle

Wilber Winkle

P.S. *While the Fifth Avenue candy bar almonds have yet to reappear, I remain quite confident we'll see them again by the dawn of the next millenium.*

SECTION ONE

———◦◦◦◦———

I'M NOT ONE TO COMPLAIN, BUT . . .

May 28, 1994

Tasty Baking Company
2801 Hunting Park Avenue
Philadelphia, PA 19129-1392

<u>Attention: Consumer Affairs</u>

Dear Sir/Madam:

I have a problem with the Butterscotch Krimpets that's been bothering me for over twenty years. I can't keep my feelings bottled up any longer and must get this off my chest. Please hear me out.

In order to get the freshest *Krimpets* possible, I always grab the package with the latest date on it. Whenever the date is one week in the future from the date of purchase, the icing on the *Krimpets* sticks to the wrapper. I'm then forced to use my fingers to spread the icing over the cake portion. Needless to say, it's a very messy process. I'm sick and tired of going through this ritual.

If I buy *Krimpets* that are not as fresh, the icing is kind of hard and crusty and separates quite easily from the wrapper. So I'm faced with a Catch-22 situation: either make a mess of myself when eating fresh *Krimpets* <u>or</u> purchase the stale ones.

If we can send men to the moon, surely you guys can invent a wrapper that doesn't stick to the icing. Please correct this problem or else I'm taking my business to Hostess.

Very truly yours,

Wilber Winkle

Wilber Winkle
5764 Stevens Forest Rd. #606
Columbia, MD 21045

June 21, 1994

Wilber Winkle
5764 Stevens Forest Rd. #606
Columbia, MD 21045

Dear Mr. Winkle,

We are sorry that you were not able to enjoy your Tastykakes.

Since November of 1989, when we replaced our icing shortening that had been composed of a coconut/palm/peanut blend with a canola/cottonseed blend, we have had to reevaluate our icings as the weather changed. Our icings have a tendency to be slightly softer. We are currently evaluating slight variations to our icing and cake recipes to prevent the icing from sticking to the wrapper.

It will be easier to open the package using the following hints. With one hand pull on the edge of the bottom fin seal and with the other hand pull on one of the end seals at the same time. Also rubbing the top of the <u>unopened</u> package on a flat surface helps the icing stick to the cake. Refrigerating the product helps to prevent the icing from becoming soft.

We hope you will use the enclosed coupons to receive fresh Tastykakes of your choice with our compliments. If you should have any further questions or comments, please call our toll free number 1-800-24-TASTY between the hours of 8:00am - 4:00pm.

Sincerely,

David W. Gunning
Consumer Affairs

#83240

August 6, 1994

Mr. David Gunning
Consumer Affairs
Tasty Baking Co.
2801 Hunting Park Avenue
Philadelphia, PA 19129-1392

Dear David,

If I understand your letter correctly, I should open my Krimpets in the following manner:

1. Refrigerate the *Krimpets;*
2. Rub the *Krimpets* on a flat surface; and
3. With one hand, pull on the edge of the bottom seal, and, at the same time, using the other hand, pull on one of the end seals.

Give me a break, David. This sounds more like rocket science than opening a pack of lousy cupcakes. I think it's a disgrace that Tastykake is raping the public in this fashion. Just in case you didn't take marketing in college, cupcakes are "impulse" products. When I buy a pack, I don't exactly feel like planning my whole day around opening them correctly.

Enclosed is a money order for $10.00 to help speed up this so-called "evaluation" on variations of icing and cake recipes. It's a good investment for me, as my nerves are shot every time the icing sticks to the wrapper.

Very truly yours,

Wilber Winkle
5764 Stevens Forest Rd. #606
Columbia, MD 21045

December 11, 1994

Mr. David Gunning
Consumer Affairs
Tasty Baking Co.
2801 Hunting Park Avenue
Philadelphia, PA 19129-1392

Dear David:

With all due respect, you are a disgrace to the consumer affairs profession. I was kind enough to offer a $10 donation for the research project to change the icing and cake recipes and you have totally ignored me. At the very least, I expected a thank-you note. I am appalled at the way Tastykake and you, David W. Gunning, are treating one of their most loyal customers.

Just to show you how loyal I am to the company, I'm enclosing another $10 donation for this very worthy cause. Please give me the courtesy of a reply this time, will you? And a friendly reminder: there are other cupcakes out on the market and I won't hesitate to change if I continue to receive this shabby treatment.

And not only will I change brands, but I'll also tell all my friends and relatives how I donated this money to your company for wrapper research and was totally ignored. And remember that coupon you sent me for the free pack of cupcakes? I'm sending it back as a symbol of my frustration and displeasure. Please find it enclosed.

I know we've had our differences of late and are not exactly on best terms right now, but I still would like to wish you and yours a very joyous holiday season. Perhaps Christmas will open up your heart and I'll get the response I so richly deserve.

Very truly yours,

Wilber Winkle
5764 Stevens Forest Rd. #606
Columbia, MD 21045

7

January 26, 1995

Mr. Wilber Winkle
5764 Stevens Forest Rd #606
Columbia, MD 21045

Dear Mr. Winkle,

Thank you for the letter reminding us about our research project that you have contributed to with a donation of a $10.00 money order. It is well intentioned but not necessary, as our company gives us a large enough budget to fund our research projects. As a result we do not accept donations from consumers.

I have enclosed your money order that you sent us.

Thank you for your communications. We hope that you will continue to be one of our many valued customers.

Sincerely yours,

Adriane Posner
Consumer Affairs
Group Leader - QA

#83240

December 30, 1995

Consumer Relations
Pepsodent Toothpaste
Chesebrough-Ponds USA
Greenwich, CT 06830

Dear Sirs:

I am absolutely disgusted with your company. I was passing my time recently by reading product labels when I saw your *little* warning on Pepsodent toothpaste. It said that you should not swallow it. How in blazes do you use toothpaste without swallowing it? Granted, you spit out most of it, but I'm sure some of it goes down the throat. And to think that I've been using your product for 30 years!

I go through about one tube of toothpaste each month. Each tube is 6 ounces, so that means I use 72 ounces each year. Multiplied by 30 years, I calculate that I have used 2,160 ounces. If just 5% of the toothpaste I have used went down my throat, I have swallowed 108 ounces, which is equivalent to 18 tubes of toothpaste! Now I'm wondering what kind of harm I've done to myself. I read all the ingredients on the label and I don't know what any of them are. One is "Titanium Dioxide." What in the world is that? Should I go to a doctor? I've had this pain in my throat recently and I wonder if swallowing the toothpaste is the cause of it.

Why didn't you make the warning bigger? You could have put one in big letters under the product name, such as, "Make sure you don't swallow any of it." I would have been much more careful if I had known all these years.

Given the fact that I have swallowed 18 tubes of toothpaste over the last 30 years, please let me know what type of medical treatment I should get. I would imagine that I'm going to have to get all of the excess toothpaste flushed out of my system, but figured I would check with you first.

Very truly yours,

Wilber Winkle

Wilber Winkle
5764 Stevens Forest Rd. #606
Columbia, MD 21045

Chesebrough-Pond's USA Co.

CONSUMER SERVICES
800 SYLVAN AVENUE
ENGLEWOOD CLIFFS, NJ 07632
1-800-243-5804

January 23, 1996

Mr. Wilber Winkle   LP   2698933A
5764 Stevens Forest Rd #606
Columbia, MD 21045

Dear Mr. Winkle:

We have received your report concerning your dissatisfaction with the packaging of Pepsodent Toothpaste.

Our packaging staff designs all containers to meet both the characteristics of the product and the needs of a majority of consumers. The warning on the package is mainly meant for children, who may mistakenly 'eat' it as candy. All of our products are FDA approved, safe for everyday use when used as directed. All packages undergo continuous reevaluation, based on changing tastes and styles, and consumer comments and preferences. Therefore, it is possible that you may see Pepsodent Toothpaste with a different type of package at some time in the future.

We appreciate your taking the time to write and have passed your comments on to our packaging division for review.

Sincerely,

Kim Wilson
Consumer Representative

kw/cl

June 23, 1996

Kim Wilson, Customer Representative
Chesebrough-Ponds USA Co.
800 Sylvan Ave.
Englewood Cliffs, NJ 07632

Dear Ms. Wilson:

It's been six months now and I *still* haven't heard from one of your doctors about what course of medical treatment I should follow for swallowing all of your toothpaste. Granted, the pain in my throat has pretty much gone away since I switched to *Crest*, but who's to say it won't come back?

I was in the store today and noticed that your warning about swallowing the toothpaste has not gotten any bigger. How many more victims is it going to take for your company to act? This is an outrage! I've got 108 ounces (almost 7 pounds!) of toothpaste floating around in my system and nobody seems to care. Have you no pity for my condition?

And finally, you still haven't told me what Titanium Dioxide is. The name alone sends shivers down my spine. I demand to know what this ingredient is.

Ms. Wilson, please let me know what medical treatment I need. Should I get this excess toothpaste flushed out? If the doctor's letter and mine have crossed in the mail, please forgive me. I just figured that 6 months was a long enough time to wait.

Very truly yours,

Wilber Winkle

Wilber Winkle
5764 Stevens Forest Rd. #606
Columbia, MD 21045

Chesebrough-Pond's USA Co.

CONSUMER SERVICES
800 SYLVAN AVENUE
ENGLEWOOD CLIFFS, NJ 07632
1-800-243-5804

July 11, 1996

Mr. Wilber Winkle   LSZ 2698933B
5764 Stevens Forest Rd #606
Columbia, MD 21045

Dear Mr. Winkle:

We have received your correspondence concerning Pepsodent Toothpaste.

We want to assist consumers whenever possible and appreciate your taking the time to contact us. Please call me at your earliest convenience at our toll-free number, 1-800- 786-5135 x 4167 to further discuss your concerns.

We look forward to hearing from you shortly.

Sincerely,

Lynn Zimmering
Product Specialist

lsz/lls

July 10, 1996

Wolfgang R. Schmitt, CEO
Rubbermaid Inc.
1147 Akron Rd
Wooster, OH 44691

Dear Mr. Schmitt:

I am absolutely appalled by your ice cube trays and I'm simply not going to take it anymore. I have two problems with the so-called ice trays you manufacture.

1. Why do you make them without handles? I get nervous when I have to carry the trays from the sink to the freezer and usually end up making a mess on the floor. If you put handles on the trays, I could probably reduce my spillage by about 50%.

2. You have no cube release mechanisms on the trays, so I must resort to all kinds of barbaric methods to pry the cubes loose. If a camera were ever to catch some of the wild struggles I have with these trays, one would think the human race had regressed 5,000 years. I twist, punch, kick, and even bite the trays, yet they still fail to loosen their grip on the cubes. The biting part hardly ever does any good, but at least it makes me feel a little better.

I'm sure there is a better way to make these trays, and I'd hate to think that these technologies are being kept a secret in order to maintain or boost current sales. I've long suspected that the public is being gouged by oil companies, and I'm starting to wonder if ice cube tray manufacturers might be milking an unsuspecting public as well. You must know that we consumers are going to keep fighting these trays and eventually break them, leaving us no choice but to go out and buy more. Quite a vicious circle.

If you are going to continue making these ridiculous trays, could you please provide some instructions on making this process go a little smoother?

I look forward to hearing from you, Wolfgang.

Very truly yours,

Wilber Winkle

Wilber Winkle
5764 Stevens Forest Rd. #606
Columbia, MD 21045

David T. Gibbons
President & General Manager

Rubbermaid Incorporated
Home Products Division

1147 Akron Road
Wooster, OH 44691-6000
216/264-6464 Ext. 2473
FAX 216/287-2996

August 27, 1996

Mr. Wilber Winkle
5764 Stevens Forest Road, #606
Columbia, MD 21045

Dear Mr. Winkle

Thank you for your letter regarding Rubbermaid ice cube trays. I apologize for the frustration you have experienced and hope that a couple of helpful hints will alleviate the problem of releasing the ice cubes.

We suggest that you rinse the ice cube trays with warm water before you fill them. There are deposits from hard water which can condense from the inside when the water freezes, making the ice cubes stick. Additionally, if you fill the trays to just below the rim of each slot, that will also make it easier to release the cubes.

I'm enclosing some new trays for you to try out. If I can be of further assistance, please don't hesitate to contact me.

Sincerely

David T. Gibbons

DTG/pb

Enclosure

April 2, 1995

Underwood Consumer Affairs
P.O.Box 66719
St Louis, MO 63166-6719

Dear Sirs:

I had a horrifying experience recently and I hold your company accountable.
I purchased a small can of "Underwood Deviled Ham" last week at the
supermarket. When I returned home to make my lunch, I noticed that the red
devil, which is pictured on your small can in 9 different places!, was holding a
pitchfork and had a very mischievous grin on his face. I thought nothing more of
the matter and proceeded to make my sandwich, which was very tasty.

When I retired for the evening, I dreamt that I was alone in an elevator. Suddenly,
the elevator stopped and the red devil got in, brandishing a red pitchfork and
smiling mischievously – in other words, he appeared the same way he does on
your can. As soon as the elevator door closed behind him, he immediately lunged
at me and began stabbing me in the chest with his pitchfork. I frantically pushed
all of the buttons on the elevator, but nothing happened. I also recall that while he
was stabbing me, he repeatedly yelled out "Spring forward, Fall back!" I can't say
for sure, but I suppose this has something to do with changing the clocks for
Daylight Savings Time. After several fearful minutes, I finally awoke in a cold
sweat.

I'm writing today not to complain about the product itself, because it's delicious. I
only request that you remove this red demon from the can at once! If you don't do
it for me, do it for all the children. From what I understand, your spread is very
popular with the kids, and I wouldn't want them to endure suffering like I have.

Why in the world do you have this menacing demon on your cans anyway? Is it
supposed to be cute? Does this red devil actually help sales? And one other thing:
Is it simply a coincidence that "Underwood" sounds so much like "Underworld"?

I hope my nightmarish experience will convince you to remove the devil from
your packaging. Until then, I will have no other alternative but to forego your
products and urge all my friends and relatives to do likewise. I just don't want to
see anyone get hurt. Thank you for your attention to this very important manner.

Very truly yours,

Wilber Winkle
5764 Stevens Forest Rd, #606
Columbia, Md 21045

15

PET
INCORPORATED

Pet Incorporated
Consumer Affairs Department
P.O. Box 66719
St. Louis, MO 63166-6719
(314) 622 7700

April 10, 1995

Mr. Wilber Winkle
5764 Stevens Forst Road, #606
Columbia, MD 21045

Dear Mr. Winkle:

Thank you for taking the time to contact us regarding UNDERWOOD Deviled Ham. We appreciate the opportunity to exchange information.

In answer to your question about the UNDERWOOD Red Devil, it is the oldest registered food trademark in use in the United States today. Both the origin of this symbol and the canning process date back to 1867, when the William Underwood family expanded their line of canned foods to meats and seafoods. Pioneering the food preservation industry, they used a family secret of exotic spices to pickle the meats. They introduced their process as "deviling." UNDERWOOD products remained a leader in processed meats and became part of the Pet family in 1982.

Thanks again for taking the time to contact us. Enclosed is a complimentary coupon which we hope you will use and enjoy.

Sincerely,

Joyce Hofer
Consumer Affairs Representative
04/09/95 6/1A 2717

JH/jh

enc: Coupon

May 19, 1995

Joyce Hofer
Pet Incorporated
Consumer Affairs
P.O. Box 66719
St. Louis, MO 63166-6719

Dear Joyce:

I am very disappointed at your response to my inquiries. Frankly, I could care less about the William Underwood family and how they pioneered the food processing industry. My only concern is the red demon depicted on the cans. You conveniently side stepped that issue by giving me some song and dance about how it's the oldest trademark...blah, blah, blah. Just because it's been around since 1867, does that mean it's right?

I understand the process of pickling the meats is called "deviling," but does that mean you have to put that evil demon on the can 9 times? Why not just address the issues I raised rather than hide behind some sappy form letter? I know I'm not the only person who's suffered because of your demon, and I'm amazed at how insensitive you are to my experience. Just think of the thousands of children who look at that demon on your can every day. Have you no mercy?!

Again, I demand that this demon be removed at once! Until then, my personal boycott of the product continues. Please let me know when I can expect changes to occur. In order to get things moving a bit, I decided to copy Mr. Marsh. I hope you won't get into too much trouble for the letter you sent me, but I feel this issue is important enough to involve the head honcho.

Thanks for your attention to this matter.

Very truly yours,

Wilber Winkle

Wilber Winkle
5764 Stevens Forest Rd. #606
Columbia, MD 21045

cc: M.L. Marsh, CEO
    Pet Inc.
    400 South Fourth St.
    St. Louis, MO 63102

The Pillsbury Company
Consumer Relations
P.O. Box 550
Minneapolis, MN 55440
United States: 800/767-4466
Canada: 800/767-5350

September 7, 1995

Mr. Wilber Winkle
5764 Stevens Forest Rd. #606
Columbia, MD 21045

Dear Mr. Winkle:

Thank you for taking the time to contact us about your experience with UNDERWOOD® Spread.

Because we are continually striving to meet the needs and preferences of our customers, your comments are appreciated.

We appreciate your calling this situation to our attention. We hope you will continue to use and enjoy our products.

Sincerely,

Sally Selby

Sally Selby
Vice President, Consumer Relations

95090600198
9509070008

August 19, 1996

James Wheat
Jiffy Lube International, Inc.
PO Box 4458
Houston, TX 77210-4458

Dear Mr. Wheat:

I originally wrote to the *Jiffy Lube* Consumer Service Department, but unfortunately they did not respond. I'm sure you are a busy man, but I have no alternative but to write to you personally and explain the problems I experienced.

Mr. Wheat, I was totally humiliated in *Jiffy Lube* a few weeks ago. While sitting in the *Jiffy Lube* waiting room, the mechanic suddenly barged in carrying the air filter from my car. Immediately, everyone's head jerked up in the crowded room, wondering whose dirty filter he had in his hand. Sensing trouble, I quickly put my magazine in front of my face in the hopes that he would go away. Unfortunately, the mechanic spotted me anyway and walked over to my chair. Sticking the filter only inches away from my face, he practically screamed out that I needed a new one. What in the world was I supposed to say in this situation, "Go ahead and leave the filthy one in there"?

After he left, I got the sense that everyone else in the waiting room was watching me. They didn't make it obvious, but I could see their eyes quickly dart away whenever I looked in their direction. The guy sitting next to me suddenly got up to get a cup of coffee, and then sat back down in a different chair across the room. It was as if I were unclean, and not worthy of being in their presence.

I find your tactics of selling air filters deplorable. The mechanic purposely attempted to humiliate me, leaving me no choice but to purchase a new one. Parading my dirty filter around the waiting room like some kind of trophy was disgraceful. From now on, if a mechanic wishes to make a comment about my filter, I demand that he discuss the situation with me out of earshot of the other customers. I can then save face by re-entering the waiting room and yelling out to the mechanic, "I'm glad everything is fine with my car."

Please let me know what you plan on doing about this situation. I'll await word that your sales procedures have been changed before frequenting your establishments again.

Thank you for your attention to this matter.

Very truly yours,

Wilber Winkle

Wilber Winkle
5764 Stevens Forest Rd. #606
Columbia, MD 21045

Customer Services

August 30, 1996

Mr. Wilber Winkle
5764 Stevens Forest Rd. #606
Columbia, MD 21045

Dear Mr. Winkle:

I am in receipt of your letter to Mr. James Wheat of Jiffy Lube International, Inc. dated August 19, 1996 and have been asked to respond to your concern. First, let me apologize to you for any lack of response from my Customer Service Department. If you would kindly send to my attention a copy of your initial correspondence, I will look into the matter further. I have checked and we do not show record of receiving your letter. It is a policy of ours to respond to every written piece of correspondence. I cannot explain the mix-up, but only apologize for it.

Secondly, I have searched our national vehicle history database and do not find vehicle history specific to you under your name. Without a copy of your invoice, I have not been able to find your history or locate which Jiffy Lube store you visited so I may address this issued further on your behalf at the store level.

What I can do for you is this, if you would respond to me with a copy of your invoice or contact the Customer Service Department at 1-800-344-6933 with that information, I will personally contact the management of that store and address your unpleasant experience.

As for our policy on replacing air filters, Jiffy Lube follows manufacturer's severe service interval recommendations. While I do not know the year, make and model of your vehicle, many manufacturer's recommend replacement at 30,000 miles or as needed. Depending on individual driving habits, some customers may need air filters replaced more frequently than others, much of which is based on the actual appearance of the filter and how dirty it is. It is not the intent of Jiffy Lube to embarass any customer in the lounge of our stores, but to educate our customers on what the manufacturer recommends based on severe service intervals for their vehicle. In this case, the Jiffy Lube technician must have felt the air filter warranted being replaced due to the appearance. However, if the presentation of the dirty air filter was performed in the manner you describe, we have a very unprofessional situation that must be addressed at the store level.

I look forward to hearing back from you with more information, including your license tag number so I may search your information expediently. Again, thank you for bringing this matter to our attention. I am very sorry you were dissatisfied with the service at the store you visited and would hope that you would give Jiffy another opportunity in the future to handle your vehicle maintenance needs.

Sincerely,

J. A. Scholl
Manager Customer Service/Systems

March 7, 1994

Alex Trebek
JEOPARDY
1040 North Las Palmas
Hollywood, CA 90038

Dear Alex:

I watched the "Teen Tournament" recently and I'm still very upset. On Friday, February 18th, a cute Jewish girl from New York was apparently ripped off. She kept ringing in ahead of the other contestants, yet her light wouldn't come on before theirs.

If you watch a tape of the show, you'll see what I mean. I'd hate to think that people are fixing game shows again. I thought we put all that behind us years ago.

Please let me know what will be done about this terrible injustice. And best wishes.

Very truly yours,

Wilber Winkle

Wilber Winkle
5764 Stevens Forest Road #606
Columbia, MD 21045

P.S. I have a good "Final Jeopardy" question for the show:
        Category: *U.S. Presidents*
        Answer: *He was so broke he had to borrow money to get to his own inauguration.*
        Question: *Who was George Washington?*
        Source: *Paul Harvey's "The Rest of the Story"*

MERV GRIFFIN ENTERPRISES

JEOPARDY!

March 31, 1994

Wilber Winkle
5764 Stevens Forest Road, #606
Columbia, MD   21045

Dear Wilber:

Thank you for your recent letter and comments regarding our Jeopardy! program. I am always delighted to hear from viewers, especially when they write to question us on specific items.

With regard to the point you raised, as I have explained on the air, our "ring-in" mechanisms are equipped with a lockout device to prevent players from ringing in too early -- before the clue has been completely read. Once I have finished the clue, the system is enabled, and players can ring in. If a player rings in too soon, he or she is simply locked out until the system is turned on. In many cases, in the meantime, another player has rung in (at the proper time). That's why on occasion, you may see a player frantically "ringing in" when in actuality it was too early, or more likely, he or she was simply beaten out by the faster player. That is precisely what happened in the case about which you are comlaining.

All our players are fully briefed on the buzzers, and have an opportunity to work with them during a rehearsal period. Sometimes during the play of the game, however, a player will get nervous and forget how the system works. Hence you may see something that looks like a mechanical failure, when in actuality it is just the player's nerves.

I hope this clears up any misunderstanding, and that you will continue to watch and enjoy our show.

Yours sincerely,

Alex Trebek,
Host/JEOPARDY!

1040 North
Las Palmas
Hollywood,
California
90038
Tel:
213 466 4487

MERV GRIFFIN ENTERPRISES a SONY PICTURES ENTERTAINMENT company

August 5, 1994

Alex Trebek
JEOPARDY
1040 North Las Palmas
Hollywood, CA 90038

Dear Alex:

Thanks so much for your gracious reply. I'm sorry about falsely suggesting that your program fixed the "Teen Tournament."

You forgot to mention when my "Final Jeopardy" question will air. I'd be very proud if you'd mention my name after reading the question. If that's against Jeopardy policy, how about giving me a little wink?

I'm very excited about seeing my question on TV and wait with great anticipation for your response.

Very truly yours,

Wilber Winkle

Wilber Winkle
5764 Stevens Forest Road #606
Columbia, MD 21045

Wilber – it is our firm policy <u>not</u> to accept material from outside sources. We have a staff of 12 that creates and researches all of our clues and responses. Thanks for thinking of us, but we are <u>returning your submission</u> to you.

Jeopardy!

March 4, 1995

Pringles Potato Chips
Procter & Gamble
P.O. Box 5560
Cincinnati, OH 45202
Attention: Consumer Complaint Division

Dear Sirs:

Why in the world do you have to make every darned chip exactly the same size? Your chips put me to sleep, as they produce the same tired routine for me again and again. I stick a chip in my mouth and wedge it against the roof of my mouth. Then, for a few seconds, I gently rub the spice off of the chip's lower portion with my tongue. When the chip becomes soggy with saliva, I bite into the soggy chip and chew it for a few seconds. After I'm satisfied that I've gotten all of the flavor out of the chip, I let it gently slide down my throat and swallow.

I'm sick and tired of eating every chip in this fashion. Why don't you put the chips in a BAG like every other brand? That way they'll break when they're being shipped and some chips will be big and others will be small. Is anything wrong with chips that come in different sizes? I'll admit it: putting the same-sized chips in a can was a cute gimmick at first, but it's been almost 25 years now! Give me a break!

And just who is that goofy guy with the mustache and rosy cheeks on each can? He's been there since Day 1. What on earth does he have to do with potato chips? I'm sick and tired of looking at him.

I'm switching to "Utz" brand chips – and your company has lost a longtime customer -- because you're unwilling to change with the times. If you want my business back, lose the man on the label and switch to a bag like every other brand. I feel I speak for thousands of Americans when I say I'm fed up with Pringles and am just not gonna take it anymore!

Very truly yours,

Wilber Winkle

Wilber Winkle
5764 Stevens Forest Rd. #606
Columbia, MD 21045

Procter&Gamble

The Procter & Gamble Company
Public Affairs Division
P.O. Box 599, Cincinnati, Ohio 45201-0599

April 10, 1995

MR WILBER WINKLE
5764 STEVENS FOREST RD #606
COLUMBIA MD 21045

Dear Mr. Winkle:

Thank you for writing to Procter & Gamble. We are concerned about
your recent experience with Pringles Potato Crisps and appreciate
the time you took to share your comments with us.

There are personal preferences with everything -- especially with
foods. That's why we do our best to find out exactly what most
people like, and then tailor the taste, performance, appearance and
other important characteristics of our products to suit these
preferences. Our product is a great favorite in today's market and
I'm sorry you aren't pleased with it.

We appreciate spontaneous comments about our products. Favorable
ones encourage us and unfavorable comments keep us aware of
consumers needs and preferences. This is very important to our
commitment of serving you with the best possible products.

Thanks again for writing. We value you as a consumer. If you have
questions or comments in the future, you may find it convenient to
call the toll-free number listed on all our product packages.

Sincerely,

Joyce Ginney

Joyce Ginney
Consumer Relations

26

August 1, 1996

David R. Cook
President, Turkey Hill Minit Markets
257 Centerville Road
Lancaster, PA 17603-4079

Dear Mr. Cook:

I am alarmed over the rapid increase of "give a penny, take a penny" dishes in your Turkey Hill Minit Market stores. It's beyond me how people can be so careless with their money as to toss it into some sort of "community chest." Even more remarkable are the deadbeats and scoundrels who think nothing of helping themselves to other people's hard-earned money simply for the sake of submitting exact change. I foresee major problems if this disturbing trend continues, such as:

1. Confusion among children over the value of money. How can I teach kids the rewards of a hard day's work when they see money being thrown around so liberally?

2. A growing dependency that "somebody else" will be there to pick up the slack when times are tough. Maybe we ought to change the old axiom to, "Close doesn't count except in horseshoes, hand grenades and at Turkey Hill Minit Markets when you're a little short."

3. Deterioration of math skills. Why do we insist on making it so easy for the cashiers? It's bad enough these fancy electronic registers calculate the change for them. Let's at least make the cashiers count the change out, for Pete's sake!

I've also been trying for years to discourage people from tossing coins into shopping mall fountains, and I'm pleased to say that hundreds of mall shoppers have reconsidered their practices after reading my brochures. I want you to know that I'm prepared to do battle with these change dishes as well, and I'm writing today to gain your help.

Mr. Cook, please let me know if I can count on your support in this worthwhile endeavor. As I await your reply, I'll get busy preparing a strategy. Thank you very much for your attention to this matter.

Very truly yours,

Wilber Winkle
5764 Stevens Forest Rd. #606
Columbia, MD 21045

257 Centerville Road
Lancaster, Pennsylvania 17603-4079

Turkey Hill
MINIT MARKETS

a Division of the Dillon Companies, Inc.

(717) 299-8908
Fax (717) 299-0519

August 15, 1996

Mr. Wilber Winkle
5764 Stevens Forest Road, #606
Columbia, MD 21045

Dear Mr. Winkle:

Thank you for writing to us in reference to the "give a penny, take a penny" idea that you have apparently seen in our Turkey Hill Minit Markets.

Upon checking, we have found that you are correct - many of our stores do have dishes for pennies such as you described. Although we have noticed these from time to time, we never really questioned their use or misuse and certainly never thought for a moment that we could possibly be creating a problem. Looking into this matter now, we find that clerks and customers heartily approve of such use because of the convenience in not waiting to break a bill or a coin of some denomination.

Despite our apparent approval of the "dishes", we would be interested in hearing more of your ideas and strategy as to how to go about changing something that seems to have wide acceptance.

We will look forward to hearing form you.

Sincerely,

David R. Cook
President

DRC/rd

28

August 17, 1996

David Cook, President, Turkey Hill Mini-Marts
257 Centerville Road
Lancaster, PA 17603-4079

Dear Mr. Cook:

Thanks for getting back to me with regard to the penny dishes in your stores. It's not surprising that your research has shown these dishes to be popular with cashiers and customers alike. Most customers like them because they can mooch a little change and thereby obtain discounts on their purchases. Put something free in front of most people and they instinctively want a piece of the action. Ever notice how, at restaurants, folks obnoxiously dig their paws into those after-dinner mint dishes?

As for the change-givers, they approve under the misconception that they are actually "helping" their fellow citizens. They deposit their loose change in the dishes and then feel all good about themselves, as if they actually did something worthwhile. They don't realize that people need to help themselves, and that sometimes the best remedy is a firm kick in the pants, rather than an endless cycle of handouts which lead to a further dependency on others.

And lastly, the cashiers approve because most of them are looking to take advantage of every shortcut under the sun. We've already given them electronic cash registers and scanners. But Nooooo, apparently that's not enough. Now they expect everybody to give them exact change to make their jobs even easier than they already are.

These dishes, no matter how popular they are, must be eliminated. It'll be an uphill battle, I admit, but with your backing, I'm confident we can win. Here's my plan:

1. Brochures, Brochures, Brochures. On the cover, we can go with the old saying, "A penny saved is a penny earned." Frankly, I don't know what this means, as it seems to suggest that money I spend, instead of save, is not earned. I don't think we should worry about this too much, because the bottom line is that people seem to really like this non-sensical saying.
2. Let's rig those dishes with an alarm to identify the scoundrels who are on the take. A little public humiliation should discourage repeat offenders.
3. As for the cashiers, fire them if they protest the installation of the alarms. Let's face it, they're not *real* workers anyway, so their ouster would be long overdue.

Mr. Cook, I'm glad to have you on-board for this campaign. As we move ahead, I look forward to hearing your reactions to my ideas. In the meantime, I'll begin to design our brochures, which, of course, I'll be sure to let you review before going to the printers. Thanks again!

Very truly yours,

Wilber Winkle
5764 Stevens Forest Rd. #606
Columbia, MD 21045

29

257 Centerville Road
Lancaster, Pennsylvania 17603-4079

Turkey Hill
MINIT MARKETS

a Division of the Dillon Companies, Inc.

(717) 299-8908
Fax (717) 299-0519

September 17, 1996

Mr. Wilber Winkle
5764 Stevens Forest Road #606
Columbia, MD 21045

Dear Mr. Winkle:

Thanks again for writing us back and telling us about your brochure idea.

While we would like to be cooperative and helpful, all we can see the plan doing is being an annoyance to the customer upon whom we rely for our existence and time consuming to our clerks for making change where they didn't have to.

With these thoughts in mind, we have to "pass" on your suggestion at this time. Nevertheless, we wish you well in your endeavors and maybe we can be more supportive at some later date.

Thanks again for writing us and allowing us this opportunity to consider your idea.

Sincerely,

David R. Cook
President

DRC/rd

30

December 2, 1995

Jim Adamson, CEO, Denny's
203 E. Main St.
Spartanburg, SC 29319

Dear Mr. Adamson:

I'm fed up and refuse to take it anymore. I'm referring to your company's ridiculous practice of "freshening up" my coffee without even asking me. I work very hard to get the proper cream/sugar balance in each cup of coffee I drink, only to see it destroyed by some perky waitress with a glazed look in her eye.

Why do you let such waitresses get away with their sadistic ritual? If I want more coffee, then damn it, I'll ask for it. I've yet to see a cook with a frying pan in his hands dishing eggs onto patrons' plates when their egg supply gets low. Why, then, are the waitresses so pushy in filling up coffee mugs every chance they get? Is this company policy, or is it simply a case of some waitresses running amok?

In each cup of coffee I drink, I add precisely one and 3/5 packets of sugar, along with 3/4 of a plastic creamer. Last night, the waitress re-filled my coffee cup when I had about half of it remaining. Fortunately, I had my calculator with me, and I was able to do the following calculations to get the right mix again: 1 and 3/5 sugar packets x 1/2 = 4/5 packet of sugar; 3/4 plastic creamer x 1/2 = 3/8 packet of creamer.

I added the appropriate amounts of sugar and cream to my coffee, took a few sips, and had to admit it tasted pretty darn good. Several minutes later, though, the waitress came back and did it again when my back was turned. I immediately whirled around and screamed that she had destroyed my coffee mix again. She ran off and summoned the manager.

As soon as he came over, I gave him my calculator and calculation sheet and asked him to do the math for me. He acted as if he didn't know what I was talking about, and said it would be best if I left the premises. After paying the bill, I did leave, vowing never to return! I have decided that it's time to play hardball, as I can't take this aggravation any longer. No more Denny's for me and my family until this practice of re-filling customers' coffee cups, unsolicited, is abolished. Thank you for your attention to this matter.

Very truly yours,

Wilber Winkle
5764 Stevens Forest Rd. #606
Columbia, Md 21045

203 East Main Street, Spartanburg, SC 29319
803-597-8678
Fax: 803-597-7505

C. Ronald Petty
President & Chief Executive Officer

December 21, 1995

Mr. Wilber Winkle
5764 Stevens Forest Rd
Apt 606
Columbia, MD 21045

RE: Denny's of Maryland

Dear Mr. Winkle:

Thank you for taking the time to write us regarding your recent visit to Denny's.

We are committed to customer satisfaction and apologize for any inconvenience you may have experienced during your visit. Your comments have been forwarded to the appropriate people for follow-up and resolution.

As we strive for restaurant excellence, we do value and welcome your comments. We do hope you will give us another opportunity to serve you again in the near future.

Sincerely,

C. Ronald Petty

November 12, 1994

Clint Fields, Executive Director
National Zoological Park
3001 Connecticut Ave.
Washington, DC 20008-2598

Dear Mr. Fields:

I and my girlfriend Luci visited your fine zoo recently. We arrived at approximately 3:00 p.m. and were delighted to learn that the zoo stayed open until 8:00 p.m. We began our tour examining the zoo's ant farm; Luci was quite amazed by this "structured community." We also spent a great deal of time looking at a bunch of germs through a telescope. This exhibit wasn't exactly my cup of tea, but Luci seemed to enjoy it. I pretty much waited patiently, knowing I still had plenty of time to see all of the really good animals.

By the time we left the germ exhibit, it was around 6:00 p.m., so we hastily made our way to "The Great Ape House." When we were stopped by a burly guard at the entrance, we were absolutely shocked. It seemed that the ape exhibit had closed at 6:00 p.m. Not only was *it* closed, but so also were the panda home and the baby elephant digs. In fact, <u>all</u> the good animals were locked up for the day!

As you might imagine, we were furious and stormed off of the premises. How would you like to go to a zoo and only see some lousy ants and a bunch of ugly germs? Why in blazes didn't you warn the patrons that the good animals were going to be locked up so early? Don't you have loudspeakers?

On our way home, I had to listen to Luci's constant complaining about how it was MY fault she hadn't seen the panda bear. She claimed I hadn't read the signs correctly about the zoo closing times. I said there weren't any such signs, at least at the entrance. Luci doesn't want to see me anymore and I think it's all because of our unsatisfying day at the zoo. I hope you'll agree that an apology is in order. Perhaps one from you will help me patch things up with Luci. It can't hurt.

And one more thing: Why do your concessionaires put so much excess salt on their hot pretzels? Perhaps if I hadn't spent so much time brushing it off, Luci and I might have been able to see the apes and pandas. Clint, I await your apology with great anticipation.

Very truly yours,

Wilber Winkle

Wilber Winkle
5764 Stevens Forest Rd. #606
Columbia, MD 21045

33

Friends of the National Zoo
National Zoological Park
Washington, D.C. 20008
202.673.4950
FAX: 202.673.4738

December 23, 1994

Mr. Wilber Winkle
5764 Stevens Forest Rd., #606
Columbia, MD. 21045

Dear Mr. Winkle:

Sorry that your trip to the National Zoo was disappointing. I apologize for any inconvenience you experienced.

Closing times for animal houses are posted at each of the entrances to the Zoo and printed on our Zoo maps.

I will discuss the excessive amounts of salt on the pretzels with my Food Service Director.

I wish you luck with Luci. Perhaps acknowledging that you missed the closing times at the entrance would help. Humility never hurts in affairs of the heart.

Please come back to visit us.

Sincerely,

Clinton A. Fields
Executive Director

P.S. I have enclosed some coupons for your next visit.

34

June 17, 1993

Hershey Foods Corp.
<u>Attention: Consumer Relations</u>
P.O. Box 815
Hershey, PA 17033

Dear Sirs,

I am generally not the type to complain, but this is something that needs to be said. I will not let your company rip off the American public and get away with it. I am writing with regard to the almond's disappearance from the 5th Avenue candy bar.

Many years ago, I purchased the candy bar quite frequently. I especially enjoyed the almond, which was lodged on top of the bar and covered with milk chocolate. As the years went by and new candy bars appeared almost daily, I must admit that I strayed and stopped purchasing the 5th Avenue bar altogether.

Yesterday, I noticed the supermarket was all out of my new bar of choice, "Butterfinger." I then scanned the candy case and spotted the 5th Avenue in its attractive brown and yellow wrapper. I thought it would be great to eat one again, kind of like bumping into a friend you haven't seen in years.

When I reached home, I poured myself a cold glass of milk and anxiously unwrapped the bar. It was then that I made the horrifying discovery - THE ALMOND WAS GONE!!! Thinking it may have been a fluke, I went back to the store to check out the remaining supply. I gently rubbed my fingers over several bars, but they were all flat. If the almonds were still on the bars, I would have felt them protruding from the smooth chocolate surface.

I demand an explanation. To simply discontinue the almond and not inform the public is horrendous. I am sure you could have kept many of your old customers like me if you had just told us. Your marketing people surely could have come up with a clever ad campaign such as, "Even without the almond, we're still better than the rest."

5th Avenue to me has always represented class. For pulling an underhanded stunt like this, your company is unworthy of its name. You have lost my business forever and ever.

Very truly yours,

Wilber Winkle
5764 Stevens Forest Rd. #606
Columbia, MD 21045

35

CONSUMER RELATIONS DEPARTMENT

Hershey Chocolate U.S.A.
P.O. Box 815, Hershey, PA 17033-0815 Phone: 1-800-468-1714

A Division of
Hershey Foods

July 7, 1993

Mr. Wilber Winkle
#606
5764 Stevens Forest Road
Columbia, MD 21045

Dear Mr. Winkle:

We appreciate your contacting us regarding our 5TH AVENUE candy bar and for giving us the opportunity to respond.

In our continuing effort to maintain products that satisfy consumers' tastes, we have made changes to 5th AVENUE Candy Bar. The most noticeable change has been the replacement of the two almond halves with additional milk chocolate. Also, the manufacturing process of the peanut butter center has been modified to give the bar a more consistent crispy, crunchy texture. Extensive consumer testing has shown that these changes to the traditional 5th AVENUE Candy Bar ingredients have improved the taste and quality of the candy bar.

We realize that consumer's tastes vary and that it is impossible to develop a product everyone will like. However, we are constantly trying to improve existing products as well as develop new ones so that we can manufacture products with widespread consumer appeal. Although our 5TH AVENUE may not be to your liking we hope you will enjoy some of our other HERSHEY'S products.

Thank you for your interest in our company and its products. Enclosed is some literature which we hope you will enjoy.

Sincerely,

Pauline E. Ward
Senior Consumer Correspondent

PW5/djl
Enclosure

July 19, 1993

Hershey Foods Corp.
P.O. Box 815
Hershey, PA 17033

Dear Ms. Ward,

I am upset and confused by your letter dated July 7, 1993. Okay, I admit the new bar has a more crispy, crunchy texture, but is this increased crispiness and crunchiness worth the elimination of the almond? I am sure I speak for millions of Americans when I say - NO WAY!

You claim extensive consumer testing has shown that the changes have improved the taste and quality of the candy bar. Just who took part in these tests, Ms. Ward? What twisted mind would prefer additional chocolate at the expense of the almond?

I have a theory on why the almond was eliminated. It has to do with money. I figure the 5th Avenue is much cheaper to produce now that you don't have to lay those almonds ever so gently on the top of the bar. Was this the real reason, Ms. Ward? Please level with me. I know you would like me to believe that the bar tastes better now, but we both know that's not true.

I look forward to your reply.

Very truly yours,

Wilber Winkle

Wilber Winkle
5764 Stevens Forest Rd. #606
Columbia, MD 21045

P.S. How drastically have sales dropped since the almond's demise?

November 3, 1993

Ms. Pamela Ward
Hershey Foods Corp.
P.O. Box 815
Hershey, PA 17033

Dear Ms. Ward:

I recently took a vacation to the wonderful city of Hershey, PA. I hoped to accomplish three things during my trip: (1) Tour the Chocolate Museum, (2) Ride the Super Duper Looper Roller Coaster, and (3) Discover the truth regarding the almond's disappearance from the 5th Avenue Bar. Two of these goals were achieved, yet I was not successful on the third, which is why I'm writing once again.

During my visit, I questioned scores of people about the almond's demise, yet no one supplied me a satisfactory answer. Most people just shrugged their shoulders and said they hadn't given the matter much thought. Amazingly, the worker who seated me on the Log Flume ride said he wasn't even aware that the bar had an almond on it in the first place. I believe Hershey needs to better train employees on the history of their products. He was an embarrassment to your organization.

I was also dismayed by the fact that after touring the Chocolate Museum, all I received were a couple of Hershey kisses. I seem to remember as a kid getting a bunch of goodies at the end of the tour, including an entire Hershey Bar. I suppose this is another cost-cutting tactic your most loyal fans will have to absorb.

I note my correspondence of July 19, 1993 has gone unanswered. I assume you are busy researching the matter. Just wanted to let you know I'm still anxiously awaiting your reply. Thank you very much, Ms. Ward.

Very truly yours,

Wilber Winkle

Wilber Winkle
5764 Stevens Forest Rd. #606
Columbia, MD 21045

January 28, 1994

Ms. Pamela Ward
Hershey Foods Corp.
P.O. Box 815
Hershey, PA 17033

Dear Ms. Ward,

A belated Happy New Year to you and all of your co-workers at Hershey! Thank you very much for your assistance last year in attempting to unravel the mystery of the missing almond from the 5th Avenue candy bar.

Since you've worked so hard for me, please accept my generous donation of $10. I feel like giving something back to the organization that has brought me so much joy over the years. I trust this will compensate Hershey somewhat for the time you've spent on the research.

I'm still anxiously awaiting the results of your investigation into the almond's demise.

Thanks again.

Very truly yours,

Wilber Winkle
5764 Stevens Forest Rd. #606
Columbia, MD 21045

March 10, 1994

Mr. Wilber Winkle
#606
5764 Stevens Forest Road
Columbia, MD   21045

Dear Mr. Winkle:

Thank you for letting us know how much you appreciate our service.
Because your words of appreciation are thanks enough, we are returning
your money order so you can share this gift with your favorite charity.

Sincerely,

Natalie K. Smythe

Natalie K. Smythe
Consumer Relations

NS/cl

1030818A

March 22, 1994

Ms. Natalie Smythe
Consumer Relations
Hershey Chocolate
P.O. Box 815
Hershey, PA 17033

Dear Ms. Smythe:

Thanks very much for your gracious reply. Unfortunately, there's been a terrible misunderstanding. Your predecessor, Pamela Ward, was researching a very important matter for me. For months, she has been trying to figure out for me why they took the almond out of the 5th Avenue candy bar. In fact, she seemed to be in the middle of the project. I assume you've taken over her task or position.

I've enclosed a gift of $10 again. I see nothing wrong with your personally taking the money, even though she probably put a lot more hours into the research project than you did. If you don't want the money, why not buy some candy bars with it and give it to those people who carry the "I'll Work For Food" signs?

Please do me a favor and go to Ms. Ward's desk and look for her file on this subject. I've been waiting an awful long time for an answer and the suspense is killing me. Once again, I need to know why they took the almond out of the 5th Avenue candy bar.

Very truly yours,

Wilber Winkle

Wilber Winkle
5764 Stevens Forest Rd. #606
Columbia, MD 21045

August 8, 1994

Ms. Natalie Smythe
Consumer Relations
Hershey Chocolate
P.O. Box 815
Hershey, PA 17033

Dear Ms. Smythe,

Just wanted to get an update on how the research is coming along into the disappearance of the almond from the 5th Avenue candy bar. If you recall, I sent you a donation of $10 back in March to help with expenses. Please let me know if research has stalled and you're in need of an additional donation. I could probably come through with another 10 bucks or so, depending on how high my air conditioning bill is this month. Hopefully, it won't be too much, as I always use a fan during the day.

Hope you're having a wonderful summer and I look forward to hearing back from you.

Very truly yours,

Wilber Winkle

Wilber Winkle
5764 Stevens Forest Rd. #606
Columbia, MD 21045

October 19, 1994

Mr. Wilber Winkle
#606
5764 Stevens Forest Road
Columbia, MD   21045

Dear Mr. Winkle:

I apologize for the apparent confusion with your inquiry about why the almonds were removed from the 5TH AVENUE candy bar. I hope the following explanation will solve this mystery.

At times we reformulate products to increase their appeal to consumers' preferences. These reformulations are accompanied by extensive market research testing to ensure that consumers will like the change.

For these reasons, our Marketing Department made the decision in 1988 to remove the two almond halves. The addition of more milk chocolate as well as modifying the peanut butter center to give the bar a more consistent crispy, crunchy texture were the result of extensive consumer testing. Research has shown that these changes have improved the taste and quality of the product.

Unfortunately, when changes are made we realize that some of our consumers will be disappointed. We are sorry if you fall under this category. Please be sure that your comments have been shared with our Marketing Department.

Thank you for your interest in our products.

Sincerely,

Natalie K. Smythe

Natalie K. Smythe
Consumer Relations

HERSHEY'S
A Century of Excellence
1894   1994

December 21, 1995

Robert Goizueta, CEO
Coca-Cola
One Coca-Cola Plaza
Atlanta, GA 30313

Dear Mr. Goizueta:

Why don't you cut out this nonsense about keeping your Coca-Cola recipe a secret from the public? I, for one, would like to know what I'm putting into my body. I don't like these games you people are playing by keeping everything hidden.

I reviewed the ingredients listed on a Coke can and spotted your clever way of disguising its mysterious ingredients. "Natural Flavors" is how you list them. I demand to know what these "Natural Flavors" are this instant!!! And while you're at it, how about explaining "Phosphoric Acid" for me?

And one more question: Why are your still running that same polar bear ad you used last Christmas? Couldn't you spend the money to come up with a sequel?! Granted, the advertisement is very cute, but I've seen it now about 200 times and I'm getting a bit fed up with it!

To sum up my complaints: If you would like me to continue to drink Coke, please let me know the product's mystery ingredients and stop running that polar bear advertisement.

On another note, here's hoping that you and yours and have a very joyous holiday season. Don't get too upset about the tone of my letter, Mr. Goizueta. I'm probably just a little wound up about the holidays and need to blow off a little steam. This is a good way to do it, as I feel much better now, and I'm sure you value the opinion of the public, of which I am a member.

Very truly yours,

Wilber Winkle

Wilber Winkle
5764 Stevens Forest Rd. #606
Columbia, MD 21045

The Coca-Cola Company

COCA-COLA PLAZA
ATLANTA, GEORGIA

ADDRESS REPLY TO
P. O. DRAWER 1734
ATLANTA, GA 30301
1-800-438-2653

January 23, 1996

Mr. Wilber Winkle
5764 Stevens Forest Rd.
No. 606
Columbia, MD 21045

Dear Mr. Winkle:

Mr. Roberto Goizueta asked me to thank you for your recent letter regarding the ingredients in our products and our holiday advertising. We appreciate this opportunity to respond to the various questions you raised.

Regarding the natural flavors in our products, flavor formulations are very valuable proprietary information; therefore, as a matter of policy we do not discuss the flavoring materials used in our products. I can assure you however, that all flavorings used in our products are approved by the U.S. Food and Drug Administration and the Health authorities around the world in the 195 countries in which are products are sold.

You also inquired about the ingredient phosphoric acid. Phosphoric acid is a compound that is naturally present in small amounts in many foods. It is also used as an acidulant in certain soft drinks, including Coca-Cola, to add a pleasant tartness to the beverage. Phosphoric acid contains phosphorous, an essential nutrient and one of the basic elements of nature.

We were pleased to hear that you liked the holiday "Polar Bear" ad, despite the fact that you felt it was aired too frequently. It is a challenge to appeal to as many consumers in our vast target market as possible. Your constructive criticism helps us know when we are not successful in accomplishing this difficult task. The 1996 advertising campaign is an exciting and dynamic one. We hope that you will find enjoyment in our new ads, and hopefully your next favorite commercial will be one of ours.

As you know Mr. Winkle, we are a consumer-oriented Company, and we value the opinions of our consumers. We appreciate your taking the time to share your thoughts with us and hope that you will continue to be refreshed by products of The Coca-Cola Company.

Sincerely,

Karlyn Kauff

Karlyn Kauffmann
Consumer Affairs Specialist

Encl.: Coupon

June 29, 1996

William Jefferson Clinton
President of the United States
1600 Pennsylvania Ave
Washington, DC 20500

Dear President Clinton:

With all due respect, sir, I find your cigar habit disgusting. A fine example you are setting for the children of this country. And please don't use that "didn't inhale" line again. I think it's very hypocritical of you to attack those poor tobacco companies while using large quantities of their products yourself. I heard you even smoked a congratulatory cigar on the White House balcony when they rescued that downed pilot in Bosnia. Is this true, Mr. President?

Wasn't it you who stated several years ago that you wanted a smoke-free society by the year 2000? Take a good, hard look in the mirror, Mr. President, before pointing your finger at others. I'm grateful to the AP's Mark Wilson for having the courage to take the photograph below. It casts you in such an unfavorable light, I'm surprised he was able to get the shot without also getting roughed up.

Frankly, I'd be rather surprised if you had the courage to personally respond. I've written before and it seems like I always get form-letter responses, which I find insulting. I'm starting to wonder if you actually even read my mail! I know you are busy, but I would rather get nothing at all from you than the traditional "I appreciate your concerns, blah, blah, blah...."

Also, congratulations appear to be in order for breaking 80 on the golf course. I must say, though, that I've seen your swing and am rather surprised that you shoot scores that low.

By Mark Wilson, AP
On the golf course: President Clinton chews an occasional cigar.

Very truly yours,

Wilber Winkle
5764 Stevens Forest Rd. #606
Columbia, MD 21045

THE WHITE HOUSE

WASHINGTON

July 9, 1996

Wilber Winkle
Number 606
5764 Stevens Forest Road
Columbia, Maryland 21045

Dear Wilber:

Thank you for sharing your thoughts about smoking. I have
received many letters from young people who are worried about
tobacco use and the effects of secondhand smoke on others.

Studies show that some 3,000 young Americans begin smoking
every day. I am very concerned about this issue, and I have
asked the Food and Drug Administration to propose rules to limit
minors' access to tobacco and to restrict tobacco advertising
aimed at our young people. I believe that these proposals --
such as banning cigarette vending machines, getting rid of
billboards near schools, and eliminating misleading ads that
glamorize smoking from the magazines that young people read
most -- will help our nation's youth to look forward to happier,
healthier lives.

I'm glad to know that you are aware of the risks associated
with tobacco use, and I hope you will share this knowledge with
your friends. Working together, we can help your generation to
grow up in a safe, smoke-free environment.

Sincerely,

Bill Clinton

February 4, 1995

Callaway Golf
2285 Rutherford Road
Carlsbad, CA 92008

Dear Sirs:

I recently purchased your "Big Bertha War Bird Driver" and I think it stinks. It caused me a great deal of humiliation last weekend and I demand an apology from your company. Your advertisements imply that everyone will hit like a pro if they use "The Big Bertha." I know it's very hard to make a good golf club, but you and I both know that golf clubs just can't be designed to perform adequately on every shot. Why not be realistic enough to admit this? Better yet, why not show in your Big Bertha advertisements some golfers making some bad shots? Do you honestly think every shot hit with this club will be a good one? I can tell you firsthand that this is not the case.

I used your club last Saturday and the ball never went where I aimed it. The club must be defective. On one hole, "Big Bertha" did so poorly that my tee-drive didn't even make it to the ladies tee. And do you know what the rule is when this happens? I was forced to pull down my pants and walk to the ball. Why don't you show *that* in one of your advertisements? After our round, I demanded that my golfmates show me the "ladies tee" rule in the rulebook, but they claimed it was unwritten, similar to taking a "mulligan" on a bad shot. Have you ever heard of this unwritten rule?

I also resent the fact that you never see the guys on TV hitting bad shots. Pretty slick editing, in my opinion. Sure, once in a while they show a ball going in the water, but that's just an attempt to make it look realistic. For every bad shot, you see about 50 good ones, and I know that's simply not possible. I think the entire golf industry is corrupt!

I'm not writing for a refund, because I think it's partly my fault I made a rush decision and purchased your club. In fact, it seems all the clubs I've purchased recently have been defective. This is simply a plea to be more honest in your advertising from now on and to stop making everyone believe they can be the next Jack Nicklaus simply by buying your clubs.

I await your apology with much anticipation.

Very truly yours,

Wilber Winkle
5764 Stevens Forest Rd. #606
Columbia, MD 21045

March 2, 1995

Mr. Wilbur Winkle
5764 Stevens Forest Road, #606
Columbia, MD 21045

Dear Mr. Winkle:

We received your letter of February 4th and were concerned to hear of your dissatisfaction with your Big Bertha® War Bird® Driver. We would like you to become a satisfied customer.

Please call our Customer Service Representative, Tim Campbell at (800) 228-2767, Extension 5584, who will be happy to discuss the situation with you in detail.

We appreciate your input regarding our advertising. At Callaway, we feel that we have created products that make the game of golf more enjoyable. We stress in our advertisements that Callaway Golf clubs help to make mishits friendlier. We understand that mishits occur and think that better clubs can help minimize the penalty for poorly hit shots. We believe that Big Bertha® Woods and Irons do this better than any other clubs.

We want satisfied customers. Please calll our Customer Service Department at your convenience so that we can help you to become one.

Sincerely,

Brian S. Zender
Customer Service Department

BZ/ljk

bz004.wpd

March 13, 1995

Brian Zender
Customer Service Dept.
Callaway Golf
2285 Rutherford Road
Carlsbad, CA 92008-8815

Dear Brian:

Thanks so much for your kind letter explaining why my ball always doesn't go where I aim it when using your clubs. I must say I was offended at first by the implication that some of my shots are "poorly hit." It took me a few minutes to calm down, but then a clearer head prevailed, and I began to think, "Perhaps he's right. Maybe it is time to accept some of the blame myself for not hitting the ball straight."

It seems that, like everybody else, I'm sometimes guilty these days of claiming to be the "victim." People are always pointing the finger at somebody or something else as the cause of their problems. You, my friend, have set me straight. I feel so ashamed for blaming your company clubs for all the miseries I've endured on the course. Let's face it, when it comes to golf, I suck!

There's one thing you didn't address in your letter that I'm most curious about. That's the rule about having to pull down your pants when your drive doesn't reach the ladies tee. Have you heard of this "unwritten" rule? Or do you think my foursome was just putting me on?

I await your response with much anticipation. Thanks again for making me see the light concerning my golf game.

Very truly yours,

Wilber Winkle
5764 Stevens Forest Rd. #606
Columbia, MD 21045

P.S. You don't need to send your response via overnight mail this time. When your last letter arrived, I found the claim ticket from UPS and figured I'd won a sweepstakes or something. I hate it when I get my hopes up like that and then don't win anything.

Callaway® GOLF

April 24, 1995

Mr. Wilber Winkle
5764 Stevens Forest Road, #606
Columbia, MD 21045

Dear Mr. Winkle:

Thank you for your letter of March 13th. I am sorry that I had to be the one to suggest that all of your shots are not squarely hit. Although this is true of most of us, I sincerely doubt that your game is as bad as you say.

Regarding the unwritten ladies tee rule, yes, I have heard of it. On occasion, I too have left my tee shot short of that not so distant measuring point of manliness. However, I must admit, I have not played by the rules and my trousers have remained waist high.

I both applaud and sympathize with you for your dedication and interest in following the rules of the game, even those rules that are not in the book. I look forward to hearing from you again.

May your drives be long and your belt remain fastened.

Sincerely,

Brian S. Zender
Customer Service Department

BSZ/ljk

bz014.wpd

August 12, 1996

Brian Zender
Consumer Service Department
Callaway Golf
2285 Rutherford Road
Carlsbad, CA 92008-8815

"May your drives be long and your belt remain fastened."
– **Brian Zender, April 24, 1995**

Dear Brian:

Inspired by your words above, I'm proud to say that my golf game has improved dramatically over the last year and a half -- my handicap has been lowered to a very respectable 14. As I address the ball on each tee, I repeat your words over and over. This is now such a regular part of my game that people often ask, "Wilber, what exactly were you mumbling when you hit that awesome drive?" I reply, "Like Ben Crenshaw, I, too, have a golf mentor, and I pay homage to him each time I play a shot."

Do you recall how frightened I was of "that not so distant measuring point of manliness," ….. the ladies tee? Whenever I stroll past those little red markers these days, I give a firm tug to my belt – just to remind myself how far I've come in such a short time. Now that I've gotten my own game into shape, I must admit it's tempting to badger the other poor saps who dribble their drives off the tee. So far, I'm pleased to say, I've resisted the urge to enforce that unwritten rule. After all, I was once in their spikes, too.

Brian, thanks again for your inspirational words and support. If you ever see Wilber Winkle walking towards the 18th tee at Augusta, mumbling a few words to himself, tugging on his belt, and wiping a couple of tears from his eyes, you'll know why.

Very truly yours,

Wilber Winkle
5764 Stevens Forest Rd. #606
Columbia, MD 21045

SECTION TWO

I WAS JUST WONDERING . . .

December 9, 1993

Kraft General Foods, Inc.
Box FP-13
White Plains, NY 10625
<u>Attention</u>: Consumer Relations

Dear Sir or Madam:

Although I enjoy Fruity Pebbles very much, I'm disappointed by your latest marketing campaign for the product. I'm referring to the Bedrock Circus ink stamps included free in each box of cereal. I note that, in this promotion, Fred, Barney, Bam-Bam, Pebbles, and Dino all have their own ink stamp. What's disturbing is the fact that Wilma, for some reason, does not.

I also note that Fred is pictured on the latest package of Fruity Pebbles. Couldn't you at least find room for *one* picture of Wilma? It's my opinion that Wilma carried the show all those years, and I thus find her absence appalling and quite unfair. Even Dino is pictured on the box. I can't believe a pet dinosaur who was such a marginal member of the cast is now getting more attention than Wilma.

Please give Wilma the credit she so richly deserves. I urge your company to return her to the front of the Fruity Pebbles box and to add an ink stamp in her behalf. Better yet, why not give Wilma her own cereal?

Very truly yours,

Wilber Winkle
5764 Stevens Forest Road #606
Columbia, MD 21045

POST® Cereals have the taste you want and the nutrition you need.

March 03, 1994

Mr. Wilber Winkle
5764 Stevens Forest Road
Apartment 606
Columbia, MD 21045

Dear Mr. Winkle,

Thank you for contacting us about our promotional offer through
POST® Fruity PEBBLES® Cereal.

Our Promotional Staff tries to make available a variety of offers
that appeal to the majority of consumers. Because consumer
letters, like yours, are extremely helpful in evaluating our
promotions, I have forwarded your comments on to the appropriate
personnel. As an expression of our thanks for your comments, we'd
like you to accept the enclosed coupon to use and enjoy any of our
fine products. Please don't hesitate to call or write again if
you have any other questions or comments.

Sincerely,

Gisele Simmons
Manager, Consumer Response

396860 / 397921 / RAH

Enclosure
POST FREE COUPON

KRAFT GENERAL FOODS, INC. GENERAL FOODS USA, CONSUMER CENTER
250 NORTH STREET, WHITE PLAINS, NY 10625

October 12, 1994

Ms. Gisele Simmons
Consumer Response
Kraft General Foods, Inc
Box FP-13
White Plains, NY 10625

Dear Gisele,

I'm furious that you've not responded to my inquiries regarding Wilma's status in Fruity Pebbles promotions. As Manager of Consumer Response, you should take the fall for the poor service one of your most loyal customers (me) has had to endure.

As you know, I'm very displeased at the direction your promotional staff has taken in recent months. The failure to give Wilma a Bedrock Circus Ink stamp of her own was, for me, the final straw. I again demand an explanation!

If you're having budget problems, I can understand, and I'm eager to help. Enclosed is a check for $10 to help defray any expenses you may incur in properly addressing the issues I have raised.

I would hate to take this to a higher level, Gisele, but sometimes you have to do what you have to do. It burns me up that you take your customers for granted and feel that some inquiries are simply not worthy of a response.

Very truly yours,

Wilber Winkle
5764 Stevens Forest Rd. #606
Columbia, MD 21045

February 9, 1997

Kraft General Foods
Consumer Response Division
Box FP-13
White Plains, NY 10625

Dear Sirs:

It's been almost two and a half years since I've last written, and I just wanted to get an update on upcoming promotions for Fruity Pebbles. If you recall, I'm a huge fan of Wilma Flintstone, and would like to know if you're planning to give her a more prominent role in the marketing of your cereal. It seems that all the focus of late has been on Dino. And I, for one, find that insulting.

You'll agree, I'm sure, that Wilma had a far greater impact on the success of the "Flintstones" show than Dino did. The only episode Dino ever starred in was the one in which he went "Hollywood," appeared on the "Sassy" TV show, and was in love with his dinosaur co-star -- until he saw her without make-up. Except for that, he was a bit player whose only memorable role was knocking Fred down and licking him in the face whenever he came home from work. And let me tell you, that got old real fast.

I look forward to hearing from you with news on upcoming "Fruity Pebbles" promotions. Please give my regards to Gisele Simmons if you see her. She was the one I was working with the last time I wrote.

Very truly yours,

Wilber Winkle
P.O. Box 434
Mango, FL 33550

February 19, 1997

Mr. Wilber Winkle
Post Office Box 434
Mango, FL 33550

Dear Mr. Winkle,

We appreciate your request for information regarding upcoming **POST Fruity Pebble Cereal** promotions. Also, we appreciate the opportunity to address your concerns.

In regards to **POST Fruity Pebble Cereal** promotions, we do not prepare a listing of upcoming promotions. We use different forms of advertising to notify the general public of our current promotional offers. Our offers appear in newspapers, national magazines, grocery store advertisements, tear-off pads and on specially marked packages.

Mr. Winkle, we are always interested in the opinions of our consumers. We consider your comments regarding Wilma Flinstone role in our promotions to be one very good way of assessing our performance in providing quality promotional campaigns to our consumers. Please be assured that your comments have been forwarded to our promotion and advertising personnel responsible for **POST Cereal**. We hope we may continue to count you among our many valued consumers.

Sincerely,

Brenda Feldman/km
Senior Consumer Representative

Enclosure: FREE POST COUPON (1)

June 22, 1993

Borden, Inc.
Consumer Response
180 E. Broad Street
Columbus, OH 43215

Dear Sirs:

Who could ever forget that classic TV commercial you aired several years ago – the one that asked, "Is Krazy Glue strong enough to keep this man suspended in mid-air?" I just loved the way the man in the commercial managed to hang by a helmet glued to a bridge. I firmly believe that was the greatest television commercial of all time.

I'm planning a stunt of my own using Krazy Glue. Before I try it, though, I need to find out if what I heard recently from a reliable source is true – that, shortly after the cameras on that commercial stopped, the glue gave out and the stuntman fell 20 feet, breaking both of his legs.

Our family reunion is being held in July at the same place we've had it in recent years. I recall there's a bridge that runs right over top our usual picnic grounds. I thought it would be a great gag to climb up onto the bridge and hang while waving to all my loved ones below.

Of course, I don't want to fall and break *my* legs, or fall on any member of my family, so I'll wait to hear back from you and get the go-ahead. Can you stand by that commercial's claim that Krazy Glue is strong enough to keep me safely suspended?

Very truly yours,

Wilber Winkle

Wilber Winkle
5764 Stevens Forest Road #606
Columbia, MD 21045

P.S. Why do you spell "crazy" with a "K"?

BORDEN, INC.

180 EAST BROAD STREET • COLUMBUS, OHIO 43215-3799

July 12, 1993

LAW DEPARTMENT
———
DENNIS H. RAINEAR
SENIOR PATENT ATTORNEY
614-225-7069
614-225-7133 FAX

Mr. Wilber Winkle
5764 Stevens Forest Road
#606
Columbia, Maryland 21045

Dear Mr. Winkle:

In response to your letter of June 22, 1993, we are glad to hear that you have enjoyed the Krazy Glue television commercial.

I have no knowledge about the health of the stuntman subsequent to the filming of the commercial. However, even if the gentleman did not incur an injury, we do not recommend duplicating the effect. Most people recognize the TV commercial as a humorous, eye-catching, but not realistic event, rather than a recommended use of the product.

We hope you enjoy your family reunion, but please do not use our Krazy Glue to glue your helmet to the bridge.

Very truly yours,

Dennis H. Rainear

DR:dtw

July 21, 1993

Dennis H. Rainear
Borden, Inc.
180 E. Broad Street
Columbus, OH 43215-3799

Dear Dennis:

I owe you my life! I took the helmet and the glue to the reunion, but thanks to you I didn't attempt the stunt. Instead, I applied the glue to the helmet, attached the helmet to the bridge above, and, because of your advice, didn't attach myself to the helmet. I first wanted to test whether the glue would hold.

Approximately four hours later, our family was in the middle of the traditional volleyball game (our side won 15 to 11!) when the glue gave out and the helmet came crashing down in the middle of the court. You should have seen Uncle Harry's expression when the helmet landed right near his feet. I thought he was going to croak! Everyone was puzzled as to where the helmet had come from. I didn't want to give myself away in case you improve the glue in future years.

In its present formulation, the glue is clearly not capable of holding a man suspended in mid-air. But I noticed on the glue package that you still have a silhouette of a man hanging on a bridge. Isn't this a tad misleading? I won't go public immediately. I'll give you guys a few months to correct this packaging flaw. After all, I'm surely not the only person who's ever thought of hanging from a bridge.

Thank you very much for your attention to this matter. I look forward to finding out what corrective action will be taken.

Very truly yours,

Wilber Winkle
5764 Stevens Forest Road #606
Columbia, MD 21045

61

February 8, 1997

Mr. Dennis Rainear
Borden Inc.
180 East Broad Street
Columbus, OH 43215-3799

Dear Dennis:

It's been a few years since we last corresponded and I just wanted to know how things are going with you. If you recall, I'm the guy who wanted to hang from the bridge at my family reunion, just like the fellow did in that old TV commercial. You talked me out of it last time, but we're gearing up for another family reunion and picnic this spring and I'm getting the urge to try once again. I'm hoping you guys have made some improvements on the product that will allow me to complete the stunt in a safe manner.

I'll make plans unless I hear back from you to the contrary.

Take care, buddy.

Very truly yours,

Wilber Winkle
P.O. Box 434
Mango, FL 33550

BORDEN SERVICES COMPANY

"QUALITY BUSINESS SOLUTIONS"

Legal Services:
James King-General Counsel,
  Employment, Benefits
John Stipancich-Litigation, Commercial
James Farmer-General Commercial

Keith King-Litigation, Labor
Sharon Post-Environmental, Regulatory
Diane Reynolds-Real Estate, Finance
Ken VanWyck-Patents
Of Counsel:
George Maskas-Patents

Labor Relations:
Keith King-Director

Security:
Joe Powell-Director

February 24, 1997

Mr. Wilber Winkle
P.O. Box 434
Mango, Florida 33550

Dear Mr. Winkle:

In response to your letter of February 8, 1997 to Dennis Rainear regarding Krazy Glue, we do not recommend duplicating the television commercial or any stunt which would harm you. Most people recognize the TV commercial as a humorous, eye-catching, but not realistic event, rather than a recommended use of the product.

Please do not use our Krazy Glue to do any stunt. I hope you enjoy your family reunion.

Very truly yours,

Shenia Miracle

Shenia Miracle
Asst. Director of Submissions

Subject: Weather Channel format
Date: 07-28-96 15:36:21 EDT
From: Wwinkle96@aol.com
To: feedback@landmark.net

Dear Weather Channel:

I just got cable a couple of weeks ago and was shocked to find a 24-hours-a-day weather channel actually on the air. At first, I thought it was a well-orchestrated gag. Who in this world, I asked myself, could possibly want to watch more than two minutes a day of weather?

The whole thing reminded me of the old Saturday Night Live skit about the mall store that sells only scotch tape. I for one really don't have a lot of interest in the barometric pressure in Des Moines or the dew-point reading in Omaha. Just let me know if the sun is going to shine in my neighborhood tomorrow and leave it at that.

Only recently did it dawn on me that you guys are really serious and that your ratings must be absolutely dreadful! I've got some ideas on boosting them a bit and giving the channel a much-needed shot in the arm. You can retain your weather theme, but I suggest scrolling the local weather forecast at the bottom of the screen no more than once every hour or so. MTV started out years ago by broadcasting music videos 24 hours a day. Now they hardly show any. I think you guys need to go in a similar direction.

Here are a couple of show ideas you can add to your mix:

1) "Weather Bloopers and Practical Jokes" – If your cameras are rolling during severe windstorms, you can capture priceless scenes of people getting caught off-guard. Viewers will howl with laughter as they watch toupees and wigs fly off bald people's heads and the bald people's frantic attempts at retrieval. For your practical joke segments, I suggest traveling to flooded areas. There, your cameras can be whirring as you speed your cars, trucks, and vans through curbside puddles and soak nearby pedestrians!

2) "As the Weather Turns" – After-hours soap opera featuring many of the Weather Channel's on-air meteorologists. Why not develop a steamy affair between Hurricane Specialist Jeff Morrow and sexy Meteorologist Cheryl Lemke? Or imagine the excitement of a shirtless Dave Schwartz seducing an unsuspecting Jill Brown. I'm sure your ratings will go through the roof!

I've got plenty of other programming ideas, but I think you should start with these two shows and expand from there. Please let me know when shooting will begin and whether or not I'll get listed in the credits for creating the shows. Thank you for your consideration and I look forward to hearing from you.

Wilber Winkle

Subject: Re: Weather Channel format – Reply - Reply
Date: 08-08-96 05:36:04 EDT
From: tanc0932@WPO.LANDMARK.NET (Beth Tancredi)
To: Wwinkle96@aol.com

Dear Wilber:

Got your message and passed it around the office for some good laughs. We've actually thrown around similar ideas here before.

Subject: Weather Channel format
Date: 08-08-96 15:36:21 EDT
From: Wwinkle96@aol.com
To: feedback@landmark.net

Thanks for getting back to me. I'm glad you liked my ideas. Do you know how long it will take for my programs to make it onto the air? Also, because you have tossed these same ideas around before, does that mean I won't get listed in the credits as the program creator?

Thanks,

Wilber Winkle

Subject: Re: Weather Channel format – Reply - Reply
Date: 08-09-96 05:41:44 EDT
From: tanc0932@WPO.LANDMARK.NET (Beth Tancredi)
To: Wwinkle96@aol.com

Dear Wilber:

I sincerely doubt they would ever seriously consider your program ideas for production.

March 7, 1994

Jim Derose, President
Hanes Net Products
Building 470
Hanes Mill Road
Winston Salem, NC 27105

Dear Jim:

I was deeply touched by your humanitarian effort of sending clean underwear to the Olympic spectators in Norway (see article below). I'm sure you knew how queasy people get when they must wear their underwear two or three days in a row. I know better than anyone. Please hear my story.

I currently own six pairs of underpants. The washing machine in my building costs $1.25 per load. The dryer costs $1.00 per load. As it stands now, I have to do laundry every six days. Because I'm only making $4.50 per hour, doing laundry puts quite a squeeze on my budget. I figure if I had six more pairs of underpants, I would have to do my laundry every 12 days, not every six, which would represent a savings of 50 percent.

I hate to be asking for handouts, but I figure I need one more than those spectators in Norway. After all, if they could afford to go over there, they must have lots of money, and aren't hurtin' for bucks like I am.

Please be so kind as to send me six pairs of XL underpants. I admire your compassion for clean underwear, but feel you should expand it to more needy members of the population. I look forward to hearing back from you.

Very truly yours,

Wilber Winkle
5764 Stevens Forest Road #606
Columbia, MD 21045

Hanes airlifts underwear to Olympic Games

Reuters

WINSTON-SALEM, N.C. — A U.S. clothing company airlifted nearly 50 cases of underwear to the Olympic games in Norway after hearing that many spectators couldn't afford to have their laundry done.

"We just couldn't stand the thought of all those people possibly having to work in dirty underwear," said Jim DeRose, president of retail operations at Hanes, the U.S. apparel manufacturer responsible for the airlift.

Sara Lee Knit Products

P.O. Box 3019
Winston-Salem, NC 27102
910/519-4400

April 7, 1994

Mr. Wilber Winkle
#606
5764 Stevens Forest Rd.
Columbia, MD   21045

Dear Mr. Winkle:

We appreciate your request for a donation from Sara Lee Knit Products.

Our company policy dictates that donations of our products only be made through authorized agencies in communities where our employees live and work.

We, however, as a token of appreciation, are sending you a complimentary garment. Please allow three to six weeks for delivery.

Sincerely,

Paula Johnson
Consumer Services

PPJ/ppj

April 27, 1994

Ms. Paula Johnson
Consumer Services
Sara Lee Knit Products
P.O. Box 3019
Winston-Salem, NC 27102

Dear Ms. Johnson:

Thanks very much for the complimentary garment you mailed. It fits perfectly and has reduced my laundry expenses by 16.7%!!

I don't mean to sound ungrateful, but I was confused by something you said in your letter of April 7: "Donations of our products (can) only be made through authorized agencies in communities where our employees live and work." That begs the question: Do you have employees who actually live and work in Norway?

If you weren't able to send the six pairs I had requested, it really wasn't necessary to feed me some line. I'm content with the one garment I received and don't like being fed misinformation. Please level with me and let me know the real reason the Olympic spectators got 50 cases of underwear and I got just one garment.

Very truly yours,

Wilber Winkle
5764 Stevens Forest Rd #606
Columbia, Md, 21045

February 6, 1997

Ms. Paula Johnson
Consumer Services
Sara Lee Knit Products
P.O. Box 3019
Winston-Salem, NC 27102

Dear Ms. Johnson:

A few years ago, I requested some information, but never received a response. My letter was probably lost in the mail or something, as I know it's not like your company to ignore letters from customers.

When you get a chance, could you please tell me if there are Sara Lee employees, or relatives, in Norway?

Also, on a previous occasion, you were kind enough to mail me a complimentary garment (which I still have to this day!). I wanted to again express my appreciation for that kind gesture.

Very truly yours,

Wilber Winkle
PO Box 434
Mango, FL 33550

Sara Lee Knit Products

P.O. Box 3019
Winston-Salem, NC 27102
910/519-4400

February 17, 1997

Mr. Wilber Winkle
PO Box 434
Mango, FL 33550

Dear Mr. Winkle:

Thank you for your recent letter to Sara Lee Knit Products.

Our records in Consumer Services do not indicate any sister division as being located in Norway.

Thank you for your interest in our company.

Sincerely,

Paula Johnson
Consumer Services

PPJ/cl

0119823A

July 27, 1996

R.J. Roberts, CEO
Comcast Cable
1500 Market St.
Philadelphia, PA 19102

Dear Mr. Roberts:

My neighbor, Chuck, called me a jackass today after seeing my cable bill. He said the only people who actually pay for their cable TV are too dumb to figure out how to get it for free. Chuck also said that all the cable companies know that smart people don't pay for TV, so they simply double-charge the fools to make up for lost profits.

Chuck went on to say that life is survival of the fittest, and that all people who pay for cable are at the lower end of the human spectrum. He predicted that if all of the large animals in the world suddenly turn against man, I, Wilber Winkle, will be one of the first men to get eaten.

Mr. Roberts, I've about had it with Chuck and I want your advice on how to deal with him. I figure I have three choices, which are:

1. Climb the telephone pole out back and cut his cable connection
2. Turn him over to the sheriff, or
3. Smack him in the face.

Please let me know how I should proceed. I look forward to hearing back from you.

Very truly yours,

Wilber Winkle
5764 Stevens Forest Rd. #606
Columbia, MD 21045

Comcast Cablevision
of Maryland, L.P.
8031 Corporate Drive
Baltimore, Maryland 21236
410 931-4600   Fax 410 931-6345

August 6, 1996

Mr. Wilbur Winkle
5764 Stevens Forest Road #606
Columbia, MD 21045

Dear Mr. Winkle:

Thank you for your letter to Comcast regarding your neighbor. We will investigate the situation and respond accordingly. Comcast aggressively pursues cable theft as evidenced in our numerous and successful prosecutions of same. Several years ago we launched an amnesty program which resulted in 7000 people turning themselves or neighbors in for cable theft. In 1992 over 1300 theft of service cases were prosecuted nationwide on federal, state and local levels.

Aside from the lost revenues and legal issues, cable theft affects the quality of service valued subscribers like yourself receive.

Let me take this opportunity to extend our appreciation and assure you that wherever we find theft of service we will prosecute to the fullest extent of the law.

Regards,

Mark Watts
Basic Product Manager

cc: Jaye Gamble, Area Vice President
       Tom Farrell, Head of Security

April 19, 1995

J.W. Marriott Jr., CEO
Marriott Drive
Washington, DC 20058

Dear Mr. Marriott:

I am planning to do some business in the Philadelphia area during the week of June 5-9, and would love to stay at your fine hotel. My only problem is I am a very deep sleeper and need some extra assistance to wake up in the morning. I am writing to find out if the staff at your hotel will be able to accommodate my special needs.

Alarm clocks and wake up calls do not help me. Two things I've tried do work, and they should cause very little disruption to the staff. They are as follows:

(1) Fill a large bucket with cold water and throw it in my face, or
(2) Have a member of the staff scream "Fire" at the top of his lungs into my left ear (please note: the scream should not be employed if it will disrupt any of your hotel's other patrons).

Each of these two methods has been separately very successful; when done simultaneously, they are even more effective.

I've written to the staff at your hotel directly, but they did not respond. I'm sorry to trouble you with this problem, because I'm sure you are very busy. Please let me know if your hotel in Philadelphia will be able to accommodate me. It's a shame my initial inquiry was considered unworthy of a response.

Thank you very much, Mr. Marriott.

Very truly yours,

Wilber Winkle
5764 Stevens Forest Rd. #606
Columbia, MD 21045

Philadelphia Marriott

1201 Market Street
Philadelphia, PA 19107

James Kauffman
Area Director / General Manager
215/625-6028

May 15, 1995

Mr. Wilber Winkle
5764 Stevens Forest Road
#606
Columbia, MD   21045

Dear Mr. Winkle:

Thank you for your note to Mr. Marriott indicating your interest in visiting our Philadelphia Marriott Hotel in June.

I can assure you that we will make every effort to wake you up on each of the mornings you are with us. Our goal is customer satisfaction and we will go to whatever ends are appropriate to insure that you have a pleasant wake up each morning.

I look forward to seeing you in Philadelphia this June.

Very sincerely,

James Kauffman
Area Director & General Manager

JK:nh

74

March 23, 1995

Mr. Seth Schofield, CEO
US AIR
2345 Crystal Drive
Arlington, VA 22202

Dear Mr. Schofield:

Congratulations on turning your company around. I know US AIR has a long way to go yet, but with you at the helm, I'm sure all the company's goals will be met.

I have a small problem and was wondering if you could help me out with it. I'm planning to see an old buddy down in Miami on Memorial Day weekend and would like to take a flight out of Baltimore. Unfortunately, I am a very nervous flyer, and tend to let out blood-curdling screams when the plane races down the runway and takes off. As you can imagine, this is very disturbing to the other passengers. Because of this problem, I haven't flown in quite some time.

I have a solution that I think will work. I wanted to run it by you and get your approval before booking my tickets to Miami. When I board, would it be possible for a flight attendant to put a gag around my mouth so my later screams will not be heard?

I myself will bring along and place on myself a set of handcuffs, as my arms tend to flap around during the takeoff phase. Once we reach our cruising altitude, I'm pretty sure I'll be calm enough to remove the gag and handcuffs. By taking these precautions, I should be much more manageable as a passenger.

Thank you very much, Mr. Schofield. I look forward to hearing your thoughts on the matter. Do you have a better idea? I know you have classes to deal with the fear of flying, but the one your company runs costs over $300. I simply cannot afford it, and I'm sure it wouldn't help me anyway.

Very truly yours,

Wilber Winkle
5764 Stevens Forest Rd. #606
Columbia, MD 21045

USAir

Seth E. Schofield

Chairman and

Chief Executive Officer

2345 Crystal Drive

Arlington, VA 22227

Telephone: 703-418-7096

April 13, 1995

Mr. Wilber Winkle
5764 Stevens Forest Rd. #606
Columbia, MD   21045

Dear Mr. Winkle:

Thank you for your letter of March 23, and for your kind comments about my leadership.

It is unfortunate that you are nervous about flying. We are aware that several potential customers have such a fear and thus we offer the "Fearful Flyers" course. I'm afraid the idea you proposed is unacceptable, in that FAA regulations would prohibit such a procedure. I would like to suggest that you take a "calming" friend.

I do hope your flight to Miami is enjoyable and that your Memorial Day weekend is spectacular. Best wishes.

Sincerely,

Seth E. Schofield

im

76

May 2, 1996

Crestar Financial
Richard G. Tilghman, CEO
919 E. Main St.
Richmond, VA 23219

Dear Mr. Tilghman:

I've got a roll of pennies that I am planning to take down to one of your banks next week and I'd like to know the proper procedures for carrying out the transaction. Please answer the following questions so we can prevent any complications from arising:

1. Do the pennies have to be rolled "heads up," or may I randomly put them in the roll without worrying about which side is up?
2. The wrapper I am planning to use was made by Brandt, Inc, in Watertown, Wisconsin. Is this wrapper acceptable, or should I get one with your company name on it?
3. Does your company prefer the ends of the rolls to be twisted, or is it permissible to simply fold in the ends without twisting them?
4. What information is required on the outside of the wrapper? (e.g. name, address,...etc.)
5. Will the bank teller be counting my pennies on the spot, or do most branches count them at the end of the shift?
6. If they do count my roll at the end of the shift, will I be notified if I miscounted and put too many pennies in the roll?
7. If I were to lose the wrapper I am planning to use, and you have an extra roll in the bank, would it be possible to roll them there on the spot, or would I be forced to leave the premises until I completed the task?

Thank you very much for taking the time to answer my inquiries. I'm hopeful you can provide the information needed to ensure a smooth transaction.

Very truly yours,

Wilber Winkle

Wilber Winkle
5764 Stevens Forest Rd. #606
Columbia, MD 21045

Crestar Financial Corporation
919 East Main Street
P.O. Box 26665
Richmond, VA 23261-6665
(804) 782-7685

Richard G. Tilghman
Chairman and Chief Executive Officer

May 16, 1996

Mr. Wilber Winkle
5764 Stevens Forest Road, Apt. 606
Columbia, MD 21045

Dear Mr. Winkle:

Thank you for your recent letter inquiring about Crestar's procedures for accepting rolled pennies. Exchanging rolled coin is a service that we gladly extend to our customers, and I am pleased to respond to your questions.

You may roll your pennies without regard to which direction the head is facing. We will accept rolled pennies in any official penny wrapper, and we prefer that the wrappers be neatly folded at the ends. Simply placing your Crestar account number on each roll will be sufficient. Unfortunately, I can't say when the pennies will be counted, as this depends upon the resources available at the office handling your transaction. Should we encounter a discrepancy, however, we will adjust your Crestar account accordingly. Additionally, you're welcome to roll your pennies on our premises during regular business hours.

Mr. Winkle, I hope the information I've provided is helpful and that you'll consider opening an account with us. For your convenience, I've enclosed several penny wrappers for your use. If you have any additional questions or concerns, please call Mr. Charlie Black, Vice President and Market Manager, at (410)986-1705. I'm confident that any of our offices will be able to handle this transaction smoothly and professionally, and I appreciate your looking to Crestar for your financial needs.

Sincerely,

Enclosures

Copy to: Mr. Charles F. Black

June 3, 1996

Crestar Financial
Richard G Tilghman, CEO
919 E. Main St.
Richmond, VA 23219

Dear Mr. Tilghman:

Thank you for your very nice letter and your specific instructions for converting a roll of pennies. With your help, the transaction was completed in an efficient, professional manner. That's not to say there weren't a few anxious moments, as I'm somewhat embarrassed to admit that I accidentally twisted one end of the roll instead of folding it. Believe it or not, the bank teller (Linda) processed the transaction anyway. Now that's what I call customer service!

Mr. Tilghman, you haven't heard the best part. When Linda handed me two quarters, I politely asked her if I could have five dimes instead. Much to my surprise, she made the exchange without hesitation. Now, I'm well on my way to completing a dime roll. And that raises a question in my mind: When it's time to convert the roll (probably in mid to late August), will the same procedures apply? I would imagine that you have to beef up security just a bit for dime rolls since we are dealing with a much larger sum of money (1,000% more) than with penny rolls.

And one more question: Do you have a lot of free time on your hands? I ask that because a lot of people say that such and such a person works "banker's hours," as if the hours bankers put in are some kind of joke. That's always confused me, because all of the bankers I've met appear to be very hard-working people.

Thanks again for your help, Mr. Tilghman. I think that you and the rest of the people at Crestar Bank are absolutely fantastic!

Very truly yours,

Wilber Winkle
5764 Stevens Forest Rd. #606
Columbia, MD 21045

79

August 3, 1996

Crestar Financial
Richard G. Tilghman, CEO
919 E. Main St.
Richmond, VA 23219

Dear Mr. Tilghman:

It's been two months since I wrote to you and I have yet to receive a reply. In the event my original letter was lost in the mail, I've enclosed a copy of it.

I had simply wanted to know if the procedures are the same at your bank for converting a roll of dimes as they are for a roll of pennies.

Also, I am quite interested in knowing a little bit about your work hours. It seems that bankers always are accused of working short hours and I wanted to know if this "bad rap" was justified.

Thank you very much for your attention to this matter. I look forward to hearing back from you.

Very truly yours,

Wilber Winkle
5764 Stevens Forest Rd. #606
Columbia, MD 21045

August 15, 1996

Mr. Wilber Winkle
5764 Stevens Forest Road, Apt. 606
Columbia, MD 21045

Dear Mr. Winkle:

Thank you for your letter to Mr. Richard Tilghman, Crestar's Chairman and Chief Executive Officer, regarding the procedure for exchanging a roll of dimes. I'm sorry you didn't receive a response to your second letter; Mr. Tilghman was most concerned to learn that the letter had gone unanswered, and he asked me to reply on his behalf. I'm glad to know that our teller Linda provided you with exceptional service commensurate with our high standards when she exchanged your penny roll.

The procedures outlined in Mr. Tilghman's previous response apply to rolled coin of all denominations, and I'm confident that the security measures in place at each of our offices are more than sufficient for any transaction you may have. Regarding bankers' hours, it may please you to know that Crestar associates are available any time of the day or night to meet your banking needs. By simply calling Crestar Direct^{SM}, our 24-hour telephone banking center, at 1-800-CRESTAR, you can open an account, apply for a loan, get account information, transfer funds and avail yourself of a wide array of other banking services. For more information about the many options available at Crestar, please refer to the enclosed *Personal Financial Services Catalog.*

Mr. Winkle, we would appreciate the opportunity to further serve your financial needs. If you would like to discuss any of our services, or if you would like to open a Crestar account, please call Crestar Direct. Our banking specialists will be more than happy to help you.

Sincerely,

William R. Hagen
Executive Services Officer

Enclosure

Copy to: Mr. Richard G. Tilghman

October 13, 1994

Claridge Casino Customer Relations
Boardwalk & Park Place
Atlantic City, NJ 08041

Dear Gentlemen:

I recently was a guest at your casino and lost a substantial amount of money. I know what you're thinking, that I lost it at the tables. But, that's simply not true. I lost $164 while sitting on the toilet seat. Please hear my story.

After several successful sessions at the blackjack table, I decided to cash in my winnings and catch the bus home. Unfortunately, I made a crucial mistake on the way to the cashier. I stopped off at the restroom to get some relief. I laid my chips on the toilet paper dispenser and proceeded to "take care of business." It took a bit longer than I expected, and in my haste to catch the bus, I forgot to take the chips with me.

When I reached the cashier booth, the cashier stared at me, wondering what I was doing there with no chips to cash in. Realizing my mistake, I raced back to the restroom and toilet, but all my chips were gone. I quickly figured out that someone must have taken them to the Chip Lost and Found, so I quickly searched all over the casino for that department. Because the bus was about to leave, I was forced to depart Atlantic City without my stash.

I am writing now in the hopes that I can recover the chips I lost. Judging from the number of people in your casino each day, I would imagine your Chip Lost and Found (CLF) Department is extremely busy. With the thousands of chips turned in daily, I'm sure it won't be an easy task tracking down my missing chips. I'll give you as much information as I can:

> **Time:** 11:55 P.M.
> **Date:** Saturday, September 24, 1994
> **Place:** Men's toilet, near lobby
> **Chips lost:** 1 black, 2 green, 2 red, 4 white = $164

I do hope that your CLF Department records the names of people who turn in lost chips, as I would like to offer my thanks and a cash reward to the kind individual who turned mine in!

Very truly yours,

Wilber Winkle

Wilber Winkle
5764 Stevens Forest Rd. #606
Columbia, MD 21045

November 4, 1994

Mr. Wilber Winkle
5764 Stevens Forest Road # 606
Columbia, Maryland 21045

Dear Mr. Winkle:

I am writing to you to thank you for your letter voicing your concerns regarding your lost casino chips. First, I would like to apologize for your unfortunate circumstances and your financial loss. I am sorry to have to inform you that no chips were in fact turned in.

Our Security Department takes customer service and the safety and welfare of our patrons very seriously. However, sometimes people enter the casinos with theft in mind. Our standards well exceed the guidelines set by the New Jersey State Police, and we make every attempt to keep these type of unfortunate incidents to a minimum.

Again, I do apologize that your chips were taken. We hope that this negative experience will not discourage you from returning to the Claridge in the future.

Sincerely,

Bob McLaughlin
Executive Director of Security & Transportation

Claridge Casino Hotel
Boardwalk and Park Place
Atlantic City, New Jersey 08401 (609) 340-3400

83

20120

March 4, 1995

English Adventures
803 Front Range Road
Littleton, CO 80120

Dear Sirs:

I saw your advertisement for a walking tour of England (attached below) and would like very much to go. Please send me an application.

Before sending my money in, I would like to get something clarified. Rather than walk, would it be OK if I brought my pogo stick and hopped around everywhere?

I also would like to know if I'll be allowed to "pogo" inside the Victoria Mansion, which is one of the places where we will be staying. If so, I'd best request a room on the bottom floor, as people have complained in the past when they get a room below me.

Thank you very much!

Very truly yours,

Wilber Winkle
5764 Stevens Forest Rd. #606
Columbia, MD 21045

March 19, 1995

English Adventures
803 Front Range Road
Littleton, CO 80120

Dear Sirs:

Thanks so much for sending the application for the trip to England. It really sounds like a lot of fun.

I was puzzled, however, about one thing on the itinerary. Day 13 of the two-week trip is described as a good time to "catch up on postcards." Why would anyone send a postcard the day before coming home? Don't you agree that Day 3 or 4 would be more appropriate, that sending a postcard home on Day 13 would be totally ridiculous? If nothing is planned for Day 13, just come out and say, "We have nothing for you to do this day – you're on your own."

Despite the apparent lull of activities on Day 13, I am still fired up to go on the trip. Before sending in my $300 application fee, I would like to get your assurances that I will be able to use my pogo stick on the walking tours. Neighbors sometimes get annoyed when they see me hopping around. I wouldn't want to get all the way to England, only to have the tour director tell me to put the stick away.

Please let me know if it will be acceptable to bring and use the stick on the trip.

Thank you very much.

Very truly yours,

Wilber Winkle
5764 Stevens Forest Rd. #606
Columbia, MD

English Adventures

803 Front Range Road • Littleton, Colorado 80120 • (303) 797-2365

April 25, 1995

Mr. Wilber Winkle
5764 Stevens Forest Road #606
Columbia, MD   21045

Dear Mr. Winkle,

Thank you for your recent letter. We apologize for not responding sooner.

We have done some checking with regard to your question about using your pogo stick. We require that our guests are suitably dressed for the weather and especially wear good water-proof walking/hiking boots for their own protection and safety, as the terrain we cover is sometimes uneven, hilly, and boggy. For this reason we cannot allow you to use your pogo stick on the walks. You would be able to use it in the driveway and parking areas at Beaumont, and also along the sidewalks. Pogo sticking however would not be allowed in the suites.

I hope this answers your questions, and we hope you will still consider our most enjoyable WALK ENGLAND tours.

Sincerely,

Judy English
Judy English

86

May 16, 1996

Blockbuster Video
T. Jack Williams, Director of Membership
One Blockbuster Plaza
P.O. Box 407060
Ft. Lauderdale, FL 33340-7060

Dear Mr. Williams:

What is the penalty for returning Blockbuster videos without first rewinding them? I'm asking the question because, if you don't impose a penalty, why consider rewinding as anything but an unnecessary, extra task? Heaven knows I've got enough hassles in my life already. In fact, the way I look at it, if I do rewind my tapes, I'm just doing a favor for other Blockbuster customers, and I don't see them lining up on the street to do *me* favors. Besides, you must pay people to do this, so why should I do it for free?

I also have to tell you this: I'm anxious to see if somebody in your store will challenge me if I don't rewind. Frankly, I don't think any of those teenagers you employ will have the guts to say anything to me, as I'm a rather big guy and lots of people say I look mean.

Again, though, before I start returning the tapes unrewound, I would like to get your assurances that I will not be penalized for doing so. I really like being a member of your club and I don't want my membership revoked.

I look forward to hearing from you.

Very truly yours,

Wilber Winkle
5764 Stevens Forest Rd. #606
Columbia, MD 21045

P.S. I'm curious: Why do you use your middle name and not your first name? You must have a pretty embarrassing name to want to hide it like that. Let me guess....Theodore? Teddy? Truman? Please tell me what it is. I won't tell anybody.

June 10 , 1996

Wilber Winkle
5764 Stevens Forest Road #606
Columbia, MD 21045

Dear Mr. Winkle:

Thank you for you letter concerning the service our rewind policy. Customer feedback is
very important to us, and I am glad you took the time to write.

At BLOCKBUSTER we realize that nothing is more important than our customers, and
we are dedicated to creating and maintaining an outstanding level of customer service. It
is frustrating when it seems like people could have put effort into solving a problem yet
they appear uninterested. Please accept my apology that situation was not handled to
your satisfaction.

At this time BLOCKBUSTER does not have a formal rewind policy. To insure the best
possible service we ask that our members rewind the video tapes before returning them to
the store. I apologize if you have been inconvenienced in any way.

Your membership is important to us. I hope you will continue to allow us the
opportunity to supply your family's entertainment needs.

Sincerely,

Skip Turner
Customer Relations Representative

June 22, 1996

Skip Turner
Blockbuster Movies
One Blockbuster Plaza
Ft. Lauderdale, FL 33301-1860

Dear Skip:

I wish you would have extended me the courtesy of reading my letter before firing off your cliché ridden reply. You kept alluding to some problem I was experiencing. I didn't write you about any problems. I just wanted to let you know that I was going to start returning my videos at the end of the tape. Judging from your response, you don't seem very interested in what I have to say.

My inquiries have still gone unanswered, namely:

1. Will my membership be revoked if I do not rewind the videos? You did state that "we ask our customers to rewind the video tapes." Is this a threat? Will my membership be in jeopardy if I don't comply?

2. What is T. Jack Williams' first name? You didn't even address this issue. I admire you in a way, Skip, for not disguising your first name the way your boss does. I mean, let's face it, "Skip" is not exactly a name to be proud of. I've never heard of any "Skip" amounting to anything in life, with the exception of Skip Carey, the announcer for the Braves. And frankly, I think he only got the job because he's Harry Carey's son. You could just as easily refer to yourself as "S. Turner." My admiration goes out to you for playing the hand life dealt you and attempting to overcome the obstacle of being born with a goofy first name. I wish T. Jack Williams had even half the guts you do. Please let me know his first name as soon as possible. Again, I'm betting on Theodore, Truman, or Teddy.

If my membership is important and you are committed to maintaining an outstanding level of customer service, then please provide me with an appropriate response. I look forward to hearing back from you, Skip.

Very truly yours,

Wilber Winkle

Wilber Winkle
5764 Stevens Forest Rd. #606
Columbia, MD 21045

March 26, 1995

Old Spice Anti-Perspirant
<u>Attn</u>: Consumer Affairs
Procter & Gamble
Cincinnati, OH 45202

Dear Sirs:

I enjoy Old Spice Anti-Perspirant very much. It has a masculine scent that really smells terrific.

Here's why I'm writing: The directions on the container say the product should be applied to underarms only. But Old Spice smells so good, I was wondering whether I could apply it to other areas of my body as well.

To be more specific, would it be all right to use this product "downstairs"? I mean, the terrain there is pretty similar to the underarms, in that it's hairy and attracts moisture. I can't see where it can do any harm applying it there, but figure I would write to the experts first to get their approval.

I really think my brainstorm is a super way to broaden the appeal of your product. If you agree, no thanks will be necessary, as I'll get enough satisfaction from using your terrific anti-perspirant in this new fashion.

I look forward to your response.

Very truly yours,

Wilber Winkle

Wilber Winkle
5764 Stevens Forest Rd. #606
Columbia, MD 21045

Procter&Gamble

The Procter & Gamble Company
Public Affairs Division
P.O. Box 599, Cincinnati, Ohio 45201-0599

April 18, 1995

MR WILBUR WINKLE
5764 STEVENS FOREST RD   #606
COLUMBIA MD 21045

Dear Mr. Winkle:

Thank you for your enthusiastic letter to Procter & Gamble sharing your compliments on Old Spice Anti-Perspirant. It's always a pleasure to hear from our satisfied consumers and your comments were particularly rewarding.

Many thoughtful consumers take the time to tell us about the unusual uses they've found for our products. We're always delighted to hear this praise and certainly do not like to discourage such enthusiasm. Still, we have a responsibility to explain that each of our products was designed for its own specific uses, uses we have researched and carefully safety tested. Because our primary concern is the satisfaction and safety of our consumers, these are the only uses we feel confident recommending.

We appreciate the time you took to write your letter and are confident Procter & Gamble products will continue to merit your approval. If you have any questions or comments in the future, you may find it convenient to call the toll-free number listed on all our product packages.

Sincerely,

Janie Rice

Janie Rice
Consumer Relations

June 27, 1996

R. L. Waltrip, CEO
Service Corporation International
1929 Allen Parkway
Houston, TX 77019

Dear Mr. Waltrip:

I'm planning a ghoulish Halloween party for this October and I think one of your funeral parlors would make an excellent locale. Are any of them available for rent? If the answer is "maybe," I can offer you this assurance: if some dead people are actually in the parlor at the time of my party, I'll be sure to close the coffins and warn the guests that the corpses are strictly off limits. I would also like to pay the funeral director to serve as party host, as those guys are always a little creepy, if you know what I mean.

In addition, I would also like to have the embalmer present for the party if at all possible. She wouldn't have to do anything, though. Simply having an embalmer there would be enough to give everybody the willies. Finally, I may be pushing things a bit, but I also thought the presence of a grave digger at the party, holding a shovel, would be a nice "extra" touch.

At your earliest convenience, please let me know how much it'll cost to rent the parlor – with some or all the "extras." I live in Columbia, Maryland, so if you have a parlor within 50 miles of here, I'm definitely interested.

I look forward to hearing from you.

Very truly yours,

Wilber Winkle
5764 Stevens Forest Rd. #606
Columbia, MD 21045

SERVICE
CORPORATION
INTERNATIONAL

Robert L. Waltrip
Chairman of the Board

July 8, 1996

Mr. Wilber Winkle
5764 Stevens Forest Road #606
Columbia, Maryland 21045

Dear Mr. Winkle:

Thank you for your correspondence of June 27, 1996. In response to your request, please be advised that we do not rent our facilities.

Service Corporation International is privileged to own and operate funeral homes and cemetery operations and take pride in maintaining personalized, caring service at each of our firms. Our properties are available to our families, therefore, we must decline your request.

Sincerely,

R. L. Waltrip

fee

July 13, 1996

Pillsbury
<u>Attn</u>: Customer Service Dept.
2866 Pillsbury Place
Minneapolis, MN 55402-1464

Dear Sirs:

I've recently encountered problems explaining the Pillsbury doughboy to my niece (age 8) and I'm writing today for advice. The problems started when Jennifer saw a TV commercial and asked me how old the doughboy was. Having just read an article about him in the paper, I accurately stated his age as 31. This confused the child because she had never seen a 31 year-old person giggle when poked in the belly.

She also questioned me on why the doughboy didn't have a girlfriend. I was at a real loss to answer that one, and I started thinking that perhaps the doughboy is gay. If this is so, should I simply tell Jennifer, "The doughboy is gay, sweetheart," or should I hold off answering that way until she reaches a more mature age?

I faced a similar problem in trying to explain Gilligan to her. Gilligan was certainly old enough to be attracted to women, yet he ran away or made goofy faces whenever Ginger or Maryann made advances on him. I explained this away by telling Jennifer that Gilligan was probably not mentally stable, as he had been stranded on that deserted island for 15 years until rescued in 1978. This hypothesis seems well supported by the behavior of the Skipper and the Professor. They also showed very little interest in those two very attractive women the whole time the show was on.

Do you have any advice on how I should explain the doughboy to my niece? I believe her questions would stop if you developed a love interest for the doughboy and stopped poking him in the belly all the time. (Coincidentally, I'm the same age as the doughboy, and I haven't laughed at a belly poke since I was six or seven.)

On another front, does Pillsbury have any plans to change the doughboy's general routine? He's been doing the same thing on commercials for thirty-one years, and frankly, I think his act is getting a little stale.

I hope you're able to help me with this dilemma and I'll anxiously await your reply.

Very truly yours,

Wilber Winkle
5764 Steven Forest Rd. #606
Columbia, MD 21045

February 10, 1997

Pillsbury Company
Consumer Relations
P.O. Box 550
Minneapolis, MN 55440

Dear Sirs:

I wrote almost seven months ago regarding problems I was encountering with the Pillsbury Doughboy and I have yet to receive a response.

Enclosed is a copy of my original letter for your review. Please let me know who has been assigned to handle my inquiries and how long it will be before I get a response.

Thank you very much.

Very truly yours,

Wilber Winkle
PO Box 434
Mango, FL 33550

The Pillsbury Company
Consumer Relations
P.O. Box 550
Minneapolis, MN 55440
United States: 800/767-4466
Canada: 800/767-5350

February 19, 1997

Mr. Wilber Winkle
P.O. Box 434
Mango, FL 33550

Dear Mr. Winkle:

Thank you for taking the time to contact us.

We are sorry, but the information you requested is not available.

We appreciate your interest in our company.

Sincerely,

Sally Selby

Sally Selby
Vice President, Consumer Relations

97021801976
9702190002

March 27, 1995

Wendy's
Gordon Teter, CEO
4288 W. Dublin-Granville Rd.
Dublin, OH 43017

Dear Mr. Teter:

Is it legal for me to buy one small drink at a Wendy's offering unlimited free re-fills, and then let my whole family drink out of the same cup?

I got hassled about this recently by a store manager who saw me getting my eighth re-fill. I demanded that he tell me where it says I can't do this and he just kind of shrugged his shoulders.

In case I get hassled again in the future, I would like a letter from you saying it's legal to do all the refills from a single cup.

Very truly yours,

Wilber Winkle
5764 Stevens Forest Rd. #606
Columbia, MD 21045

DavCo Restaurants, Inc.

Polly Albright
Vice President, Marketing

April 10, 1995

Mr. Wilber Winkler
5764 Stevens Forrest Road, #606
Columbia, MD 21045

Dear Mr. Winkler:

This is in response to your letter about your experience with our Wendy's Free Drink Refill program and your being "hassled" when you requested your eighth free refill.

Is it legal to refill eight times? I'm not sure "legal" is the word I would use. The refill program was specifically designed as our way of offering added value and thanking you for patronizing our Wendy's. However, the program was never intended to quench the thirst of an entire group of people with one cup. The drink cup clearly states "Free Drink Refill", meaning one refill per cup. It was more than generous of our manager to accommodate so many requests from you. I'm sorry you misunderstood.

Mr. Winkler, we appreciate your letter; it's always good to know what our guests are thinking. If you feel the need to discuss this matter further, please do not hesitate to call me.

Sincerely,

DAVCO RESTAURANTS, INC.

Polly Albright
Vice President, Marketing

cc: Joe Cunnane
      Barry Barnhart
      Michelle Torres

WINKLE.LET

June 22, 1996

Polly Albright, VP Marketing
DavCo Restaurants, Inc.
1657 Crofton Boulevard
Crofton, MD 21114

Dear Ms. Albright:

I haven't stopped thinking about your response letter to me of 14 months ago, and I must say I'm still a little upset. First, you got my name wrong. It's Winkle, not Winkler. You must have gotten me confused with Henry Winkler, who played Fonzie on *Happy Days*.

Second, your response to my inquiry on the legality of getting eight drink re-fills was unconvincing. Realizing you had no leg to stand on legally, you cleverly shifted the debate from law to ethics. Reading between the lines, I got the impression that you were sending me a message of, "Hey tightwad, why don't you *pay* for your drinks?"

I don't like to make trouble and, since receiving your letter last year, I've resisted the urge to get multiple re-fills, although I still think I'm legally entitled to them. That said, you need to know that my problems with the Wendy's Manager have started to heat up again.

The latest episode involves those tiny plastic ketchup containers. Recently, I got a carry-out order, and while in the process of filling the containers at the fixin' bar, the Manager barged out of the kitchen yelling, "You can't possibly use all of that ketchup on one burger." Counting the containers aloud, one-by-one, he told me quite emphatically, "Thirty-four is entirely too many for one customer." I calmly demanded that he show me in writing what my ketchup limitation was, yet he was not able to do so. Personally, I think he's out to get me. Don't you think he's being awful petty in counting the number of ketchup containers I take?

Ms. Albright, to avoid future hostilities, would you please let me know what my per burger limit on ketchup is? I think it's embarrassing to all of us that it's come down to this, but things will go much smoother in future visits if we reach common ground now. I'm willing to abide by whatever number you choose, as I trust you'll be fair in rendering a decision. I look forward to hearing from you, Ms. Albright.

Very truly yours,

Wilber Winkle

Wilber Winkle
5764 Stevens Forest Rd. #606
Columbia, MD 210451

cc: Dave Thomas

March 10, 1997

Mr. Wilber Winkle
P.O. Box 434
Mango, Florida 33550

Dear Mr. Winkle:

Thank you for your recent comments informing us of an unpleasant experience at Wendy's. We always appreciate hearing from our customers. We are very sorry this happened, Mr. Winkle, as it sounds like you experienced some undue frustration.

Customer service is Wendy's first priority. Keeping you satisfied is the primary responsibility of our restaurant personnel. Rude treatment of a customer or inappropriate behavior is a mistake that none of our people can afford to make. Without customers, we simply would not be in business.

Mr. Winkle, if you would, please contact my at your convenience at (800)726-6989 so that we may discuss this situation further. Your confidence in Wendy's is very important to us.

Sincerely,

WENDY'S INTERNATIONAL, INC.

Esau Sims
Division Vice President

ES:sar

May 1, 1996

Micky Arison, CEO
Carnival Cruise Lines
3655 N.W. 87th Ave
Miami, FL 33178-2428

Dear Mr. Arison,

I'm very excited about taking my first cruise. I'm about to book on the ship *Fascination* for a trip to the Southern Caribbean scheduled to depart San Juan on August 10th.

I never thought I'd have the opportunity to take a cruise, but then I read the conditions in the back of your manual. Its "Guests With Special Needs" section says, "Animals are permitted on board ships if prior arrangements have been made at time of booking." I think it's great that you guys realize how important pets are in some people's lives. I just couldn't stand the thought of leaving Clyde home for a week while I'm whooping it up in the Caribbean.

Just so you can make the necessary arrangements prior to sailing, let me tell you a little bit about Clyde. He's a 5'3", 278 pound gorilla. Though he's a strict vegetarian, no special diet arrangements need be made for him. I'm sure your salad bars will suit him just fine. I understand that at dinner one night during the cruise, dress is formal, and initially I thought that could pose a small problem. But I decided we would simply order room service that night. Frankly, Clyde would be a laughing stock if I paraded him through the dining room in one of my old suits, and I refuse to subject him to that kind of ridicule. Clyde likes it when you laugh *with* him, but laughing *at* him is a whole different story.

Although we haven't cruised before, Clyde will likely want to stay in his cabin for most of the journey. An afternoon stroll on deck will probably be the extent of his outside-the-room activities. Because he's very well trained, I'm confident Clyde will be a model passenger. He might well become a hit with the kids, too. And, perhaps with a little coaxing, he might even agree to take part in one of your shows.

Please let me know what procedures I'll need to follow to bring Clyde along. I'm sure his veterinarian will be happy to supply you his medical history in case you need it for the files. Thanks very much. I'm probably going to book my cruise at the end of May, so a swift response would be most appreciated.

Very truly yours,

Wilber Winkle
5764 Stevens Forest Rd. #606
Columbia, MD 21045

ADOLFO M. PEREZ
Director
Reservations Sales

May 17, 1996

Mr. Wilber Winkle
5764 Stevens Forest Road #606
Columbia, MD 21045

Dear Mr. Wilber:

Mr. Arison forwarded your letter to me for my responses since I am directly responsible for the operation of the reservations sales department.

Although we would be honored to have you sail aboard one of our "Fun Ships", we regret that your gorilla, Clyde, can not be accommodated aboard any of our ships. The section in our brochure to which you refer in your letter regarding "Guests with Special Needs", refers to those guests requiring the use of a service animal (e.g., seeing-eye dog).

We hope that you can make arrangements to have Clyde stay with someone so that you can enjoy a cruise aboard a Carnival "Fun Ship" in the near future. Thank you for your interest in Carnival Cruise Lines.

Sincerely,

cc: Mr. Micky Arison

CARNIVAL CRUISE LINES, CARNIVAL PLACE, 3655 NW 87 AVENUE, MIAMI, FLORIDA 33178-2428
EXECUTIVE OFFICES: (305) 599-2600   1-800-327-7373

Sniffing out nuts and Butterfingers in Congress

By Nanci Hellmich
USA TODAY

Now the sweetest secrets of Washington, D.C., insiders are out — where they stash their favorite candy:

▶ Rep. Lynn Schenk, D-Calif., tucks Reese's Peanut Butter Cups in the plants in her office.

▶ Rep. Joe Skeen, R-N.M., has a secret file drawer for Peanut M&Ms.

▶ Rep. Robert Walker, R-Pa., keeps Hershey's Milk Chocolate Bars behind his desk.

These are the findings of a survey conducted by the National Confectioners Association and Chocolate Manufacturers Association.

Questionnaires were sent to 100 Senate offices and 435 House offices; 160 survey cards were completed and returned by congressional staff.

And what do senators keep under wraps?

▶ Sen. Conrad Burns, R-Mont., M&Ms and fudge with nuts.

▶ Sen. Wendell Ford, D-Ky., Three Musketeers.

▶ Sen. John Chafee, R-R.I., Butterfingers and Three Musketeers.

Even when it's not Halloween, a lot of people will have a bowl of treats for others and "keep their favorite candy hidden away," says Larry Graham, president of both groups.

The survey also asked congressional staffers what kind of candy the Clinton administration brings to mind. One of the more common responses: Three Musketeers for Bill, Al and Hillary.

Other answers: Mr. Goodbar, Hot Tamales, Milk Duds, Payday, Junior Mints and Atomic Fire Balls.

March 21, 1994

The Honorable Joe Skeen
Member of Congress
Rayburn House Office Building
Room 2367
Washington, DC 20510

Dear Congressman Skeen:

Just wanted to let you know that I'm a big fan of yours and am proud of your many accomplishments in the House of Representatives. My admiration grew even stronger when I read recently that you have a secret file drawer of peanut M&Ms.

I've enclosed some literature I received from the good folks at M&M/MARS. It makes for some very fascinating light reading that I hope you will enjoy. Did you know, for example, that peanut M&Ms are made in equal numbers of colors? (I always thought there were more yellow ones.)

By the way, I like to put my M&Ms in the freezer. Then, when they're nice and frozen, I eat them with a cold glass of milk. Please let me know how many M&Ms you eat each day. Do you buy the ½ pound bags, or do you prefer the smaller packs from the vending machines?

The next time I'm in Washington, I'd like to stop by for a visit . Perhaps you'll let me grab a handful out of that secret file drawer.

Please let me know when's a good time to visit. And keep up the good work!

Very truly yours,

Wilber Winkle
5764 Stevens Forest Rd. #606
Columbia, MD 21045

August 12, 1994

The Honorable Representative Joe Skeen
Rayburn House Office Building
Room 2367
Washington, DC 20515

Dear Representative Skeen:

I am very disappointed that you felt my letter of March 24, 1994 was unworthy of a response. It's a shame you don't consider your constituents very important. I've got friends in New Mexico, many of whom helped put you in office. I talked to a few of them recently and they told me my letter from you probably had gotten lost in the mail. For that reason, I'm giving you the benefit of the doubt, and writing again.

Once again, my questions are as follows:

1. How many M&M's do you eat each day?
2. Do you buy 1/2 pound packs, or do you prefer the smaller packs in vending machines?
3. Can we do lunch? Third week in September works for me.

Very truly yours,

Wilber Winkle
5764 Stevens Forest Rd. #606
Columbia, MD 21045

cc: Bill Clinton

2367 RAYBURN HOUSE OFFICE BUILDING
WASHINGTON, DC 20515-3102
(202) 225-2365

COMMITTEE ON
APPROPRIATIONS

SUBCOMMITTEES:
VICE-CHAIRMAN
RURAL DEVELOPMENT, AGRICULTURE,
AND RELATED AGENCIES
━━━
DEFENSE

DISTRICT OFFICES:
FEDERAL BUILDING
ROSWELL, NM 88201
(505) 622-0055

1065-B, SOUTH MAIN
SUITE A
LAS CRUCES, NM 88005
(505) 527-1771

SUZANNE EISOLD
CHIEF OF STAFF

Congress of the United States

House of Representatives

JOE SKEEN

2D DISTRICT, NEW MEXICO

September 12, 1994

Mr. Wilber Winkle
5764 Stevens Forest Road #606
Columbia, Md.   21045

Dear Wilber:

Please find enclosed a copy of the letter sent to you on **April 19, 1994** in response to your letter dated March 24, 1994. I am sorry that you did not receive this letter and in turn felt the need to send your letter of disappoint dated August 11, 1994. With the current exposure of the problem of delivery of mail in the D.C. area I am certain you understand that you may very well have been one of those who did not receive all of your intended mail. Thank you for your graciousness in granting me the benefit of the doubt. I do have to wonder at your need to send a copy to the President!!

Sincerely,

JOE SKEEN
Member of Congress

JS:se

106

DISTRICT OFFICES:
FEDERAL BUILDING
ROSWELL, NM 88201
(505) 622-0055

1065-B, SOUTH MAIN
SUITE A
LAS CRUCES, NM 88005
(505) 527-1771

SUZANNE EISOLD
CHIEF OF STAFF

COMMITTEE ON
APPROPRIATIONS

SUBCOMMITTEES:
VICE-CHAIRMAN
AGRICULTURE, RURAL DEVELOPMENT,
AND RELATED AGENCIES
—
DEFENSE

Congress of the United States
House of Representatives

JOE SKEEN
2D DISTRICT, NEW MEXICO

April 19, 1994

Mr. Wilber Winkle
5764 Stevens Forest Road #606
Columbia, MD 21045

Dear Wilber:

Thank you for your kind letter and it is nice to know there are other M&M lovers out there. M&M's is a vice that brings me great pleasure.

I was unaware that the colors of peanut M&M's are made in equal numbers and I agree there seems to be more of the yellow ones! I have not tried your suggestion of putting the M&M's in the freezer but trust me I intend to try it. As to the amount of M&M's I consume in any one day - it varies. When times are busy needless to say I do not have the opportunity to spend much time in my office indulging but when I do have the time I can over indulge in a big hurry.

I would be happy to have you stop by sometime when you are in the District I would enjoy an M&M break with you.

Sincerely,

JOE SKEEN
Member of Congress

JS:se

March 24, 1994

The Honorable Senator Conrad Burns
Dirksen Office Bldg.
RM SD 183
Washington, DC 20510

Dear Senator Burns:

I've been a great admirer of yours for quite some time and I'd like to take this opportunity
to congratulate you on your many accomplishments in the Senate.

I read recently in the *USA Today* that your favorite candies are M&Ms. Enclosed is some
literature I received from their manufacturer, M&M/MARS. I thought you would get a
kick out of reading it. I always wondered why there were more browns than any other
color. It turns out that brown is the most suitable and pleasing color for a chocolate
product. For that reason, 30 percent of all M&Ms are brown.

I'm anxious to learn exactly how many M&Ms you eat each day. Do you have a file
drawer like Joe Skeen does? Do you eat them with a cold glass of milk like I do?

I'd love to pay you a visit the next time I'm in D.C. Why not get your aides to schedule
something for the third week in April? We can do lunch and have some M&Ms for
dessert. I'll keep my calendar open.

Looking forward to hearing from you, Conrad, and best wishes.

Very truly yours,

Wilber Winkle
5764 Stevens Forest Rd. #606
Columbia, MD 21045

P.S. The next time you're in Rep. Lynn Schenk's office, check her plants. She keeps her
stash of Reese's peanut butter cups there.

August 12, 1994

The Honorable Senator Conrad Burns
Dirksen Office Building
Room 183
Washington, DC 20510

Dear Senator Burns:

I 'm very disappointed that you felt my letter of March 24, 1994 was not worthy of a response. It's a shame you do not feel your constituents are very important. I've got friends in Montana, many of whom helped put you in office. I talked to a few of them recently and they told me my letter probably was lost in the mail. For that reason, I'm giving you the benefit of the doubt, and writing again.

Once again, my questions are as follows:

1. How many M&M's do you eat each day?
2. Do you buy 1/2 pound packs, or do you prefer the smaller packs in vending machines?
3. Can we do lunch? Third week in September works for me.

Very truly yours,

Wilber Winkle
5764 Stevens Forest Rd. #606
Columbia, MD 21045

cc: Bill Clinton

COMMITTEES:
APPROPRIATIONS
COMMERCE, SCIENCE, AND
TRANSPORTATION
SMALL BUSINESS
SPECIAL COMMITTEE ON AGING

United States Senate

WASHINGTON, DC 20510–2603

September 22, 1994

Wilber Winkle
5764 Stevens Forest Road #606
Columbia, Maryland   21045

Dear Wilber:

Thank you for following up on your "M&M survey." I apologize for not responding to your first note. Since early spring Montanans have been writing and calling me in record numbers, and I think a note like yours from Maryland just slipped through the cracks. I'm having a tough time just keeping up with the folks from home!

To answer your questions, though, I eat one pack of M&M's each day and I prefer the smaller packs. I can't tell you where I hide my stash, since my staff is likely to read this and, Lord knows, I don't want them finding out.

You asked about having lunch and I would love to. If you can wait til after the election, that would be best with me. As I'm sure your friends in Montana have told you, I've got a tough race and I'm spending every free moment back home. But if you want to give my office a call after November, I'd be happy to do lunch.

I appreciate your persistence and your patience, Wilber. I don't think any letter I receive is not worthy of response. Unfortunately, it comes down to time, or I should say lack of time. But I look forward to seeing you later this fall.

With best wishes,

Sincerely,

Conrad Burns
United States Senator

CRB/pad

110

July 12, 1993

McDonalds Corporation
McDonald's Plaza
Oak Brook, IL 60521

Dear Sirs:

Where is Ronald McDonald? I haven't seen him in your commercials for years.

I had expected to see him resurface when the Big Mac celebrated its 25th anniversary, but he was suspiciously absent from all the festivities.

What causes me concern is that I've heard from a reliable source that Ronald has cancer and is unable to make public appearances. I sure hope that's not the case, but, if it is, please send me an address where I can send him a get-well card.

Very truly yours,

Wilber Winkle
5764 Stevens Forest Road #606
Columbia, MD 21045

P.S. Please send me the recipe for the Big Mac sauce.

McDonald's Corporation
McDonald's Plaza
Oak Brook, Illinois 60521
Direct Dial Number

(708) 575-6198

August 6, 1993

Mr. Wilber Winkle
5764 Stevens Forest Road #606
Columbia, MD   21045

Dear Mr. Winkle:

Thank you for writing McDonald's with your questions about Ronald McDonald.

First, I want to assure you that Ronald McDonald is alive and well, travelling all over the world visiting his favorite people... children! He also keeps busy making appearances in Saturday morning McDonald's commercials. And, now that we operate restaurants in 66 countries, Ronald McDonald is busier than ever exploring new and exotic places all over the world and making more public appearances than he ever has before.

He also tries to pop-up at your local McDonald's from time to time...perhaps you'll see him there soon. Ronald is glad to know that you're looking out for him, and he asked me to give you his photograph, which he autographed just for you.

Again, Mr. Winkle, thank you for expressing your interest in Ronald McDonald. Please use the enclosed gift certificates on your next visit to one of our restaurants. We hope to serve you soon.

Sincerely,

McDONALD'S CORPORATION

Carol Lareau
Representative
Customer Satisfaction Department

Enclosures

P.S.   We're unable to reveal the <u>secret</u> recipe for the Big Mac sauce -- it's part of what makes coming to McDonald's a unique experience!

July 14, 1996

Ronald McDonald
McDonald's Corporation
McDonald's Plaza
Oak Brook, IL 60521

Dear Ronald:

What's new, you red headed goofball? Only kidding, Ronald. A little good-natured ribbing is healthy for any friendship, don't you? I know you like to dish it out yourself, so go ahead and fire away at me, OK? I have some freckles on my face, so you may want to use that as fodder for a really good comeback.

Believe it or not, it's been three years since you sent me that autographed picture. I'm dying to know what you're up to these days. I also have a question, Ronald: Why doesn't McDonald's count the number of burgers served anymore? Unfortunately, all the signs now read "billions and billions served." When I see "billions and billions served," it's like McDonald's is saying, "Do you really expect us to keep climbing up these signs each week like a bunch of gorillas just to change the number?"

Well, frankly Ronald, I do. After all, you've got a pretty good business going, and I don't think this is too much to ask in return. Please have a talk with the Managers and tell them to put the numbers up again. I would imagine you have a fair amount of pull in the organization, so I'm sure they'll do it if you tell them to.

I hope to hear from you again, you crazy clown. And don't forget to pick on me about my freckles.

Very truly yours,

Wilber Winkle

Wilber Winkle
5764 Stevens Forest Rd. #606
Columbia, MD 21045

Ronald McDonald®

Hi, Wilber:

Thanks for your great letter. I love to hear from my friends.

I also love my job at McDonald's because I get to be with my favorite people, children. Since I came to McDonaldland in 1969, I've been very busy visiting with children all over the world. When I'm not traveling, I live with my friends in McDonaldland -- Grimace, Hamburglar, Birdie, the Fry Kids, the Happy Meal Guys, CosMc and the McNugget Buddies.

Wilber, I think it's great that you have freckles on your face! They're just one of the things that make you special. I wouldn't mind having a few freckles myself. I think they'd go great with my bright red hair. What do you think?

You asked why we're not counting hamburgers anymore. Hmmm...let me think. Maybe it's because the person who was counting ran out of breath! Or, maybe the person who was counting retired and they've been having a hard time finding a new "official burger counter"...maybe the "official burger counter" is still flying around the world and hasn't yet returned to tally and post the numbers. Whatever the reason, I know for sure we're over 100 billion served.

Well, it's time to round up the gang for lunch. Mmm...I think I'll have a hamburger, some golden french fries, and a creamy chocolate shake. I can hardly wait!

'Til we meet, I'm your very own clown.

Your pal,

Ronald McDonald

August 2, 1996

Ronald McDonald
McDonald's Corporation
McDonald's Plaza
Oak Brook, IL 60521

Dear Mr. McDonald:

Thanks for your letter. Yes, I agree, freckles would go great with your bright red hair. I also thought it was very funny when you said the burger counter ran out of breath counting all of the burgers sold. I was laughing so hard I almost fell out of my chair.

Ronald, I'm still a little confused about one thing, though. I recently saw some commercials where you were playing golf and dancing in discotheques with other adults. Ever since the *Arch Deluxe* came out, it seems you've been acting differently. You don't joke around as much as you used to, and when I saw you on the golf course, you seemed extremely serious. In fact, you didn't smile once in the whole commercial.

If it's true that you're spending all your time now with adults, why did you state in your letter to me that you still live with Grimace, Hamburglar, Birdie, the Fry Kids, the Happy Meal Guys, CosMc and the McNugget Buddies? They all seem pretty immature to me, and I think you should move out of McDonaldland if you really want the friendship of other adults. I'm sure all the kids are going to miss you, but you're 27 years-old now, and I guess it's only natural to want to spend more time with people your own age.

Thanks for everything, Mr. McDonald. I'll always be your pal.

Very truly yours,

Wilber Winkle

Wilber Winkle
5764 Stevens Forest Rd. #606
Columbia, MD 21045

McDonald's Corporation
McDonald's Plaza
Oak Brook, Illinois 60521
Direct Dial Number

(630) 575-6198

August 12, 1996

Mr. Wilber Winkle
5764 Stevens Forest Road #606
Columbia, MD 21045

Dear Mr. Winkle:

Ronald McDonald has asked me to respond to your letter of August 2. I want to thank you for writing and sharing your thoughts with him. I'm also glad you found his recent response entertaining and enjoyable. After all, Ronald loves to make people laugh!

As you know, Ronald is no ordinary clown. He's unique because he appeals to both children and adults. He's completely comfortable engaging in adult activities such as golf and disco dancing, but can also hang out with his best buddies in McDonaldland. That's Ronald's special gift--the ability to transcend both worlds to bring out the best in children and adults. That's the makings of an all-around clown!

Mr. Winkle, I hope we've cleared your confusion up. I'll share your comments with Ronald the next time I see him. I'm sure he'll appreciate them.

Thank you again for your letter.

Sincerely,

McDONALD'S CORPORATION

Marisa Fernandez
Representative
Customer Satisfaction Department

August 19, 1996

Forster Inc.
P.O. Box 657
Witton, Maine 04294

Dear sirs:

Just wanted to drop you a quick note to let you know how thrilled I am to have discovered your wonderful toothpicks. I change toothpick brands more often than some people change socks, and I'm excited that I've finally found one that does such a fantastic job. Forster toothpicks fit comfortably between my fingers and have a very fine texture compared to other brands, which were rather coarse and a bit rough on my fingers.

If I can manage to save enough money, I'd like to visit the factory where your toothpicks are manufactured. I'm sure it's a fascinating place and a fascinating process.

Please send information on when tours are conducted and let me know if any hotels in the area offer package deals that include factory tours.

I would also greatly appreciate any other literature you may have that will enable me to learn more about your product and manufacturing process.

Thank you very much and I look forward to hearing back from you.

Very truly yours,

Wilber Winkle
5764 Stevens Forest Road #606
Columbia, MD 21045

August 22, 1996

Wilber Winkle
5764 Stevens Forest Rd. #606
Columbia, MD 21045

Dear Mr. Winkle:

Thank you for your letter regarding your appreciation for the Forster toothpick. We appreciate it when a customer takes the time to contact Forster Inc. with questions or comments.

Per your request I have enclosed some literature on the toothpick manufacturing process. Also you will find a history sheet on how Forster was born 109 years by the toothpick. In answer to your questions on plant tours, our company use to conduct them, but however we no longer do. I have enclosed some samples of our flavored toothpicks as well. Enjoy!

Again, thank you for contacting Forster Inc.

Sincerely,

(Ms.) Tracie D. Elliott
Consumer Inquiries/ Purchasing Associate

/te
encl.

August 8, 1996

M. Anthony Burns, CEO
Ryder Trucks
3600 NW 82nd Ave.
Miami, FL 33166

Dear Mr. Burns:

I am moving to Florida because I figure the climate is much better down there for my pet, Clyde. It's also why I'm writing you at Ryder. Although I have very little furniture to transport on my upcoming move from Maryland to Florida, I need a rather large truck because I want Clyde to be as comfortable as possible during the long trip.

Please answer the following questions so I can determine if a Ryder truck will be suitable for my move:

1. Is there ventilation in the back of your trucks? I suppose if it got too hot back there, Clyde could sit up front with me, but people tend to stare a lot when I have him alongside in the car, and I'd like to avoid such staring if at all possible.
2. Are the walls on the truck sturdy? Clyde throws an occasional temper tantrum and I wouldn't want him to cause any damage. Rest assured, I'll have plenty of bananas on hand, as they tend to calm down the rascal when he gets in one of his moods.
3. What's the largest truck I can get with automatic transmission? I can drive a stick OK, but I tend to be a little jerky with it at times and I'm afraid Clyde might get upset if the ride isn't smooth.
4. Would it be possible to get some assistance when securing Clyde in the back of the truck? He's usually very agreeable, yet it may take three or four of us to get him in there if he decides to put up a struggle.

Mr. Burns, I know you're probably thinking that I'm a worry-wart for asking all these questions, but I like to be prepared for anything.

Please address my concerns as soon as possible. My move is now about 45 days away.

Thank you.

Very truly yours,

Wilber Winkle

Wilber Winkle
5764 Stevens Forest Rd.#606
Columbia, MD 21045

Ryder Consumer Truck Rental
3600 NW 82 Avenue
Miami, Florida 33166

August 26, 1996

Mr. Wilber Winkle
5764 Stevens Forest Road
606
Columbia, MD 21045

RYDER

Dear Mr. Winkle,

I would like to acknowledge your letter to Mr. Anthony Burns, Chairman, President and CEO of Ryder System, Inc. As I am responsible for customer service matters, Mr. Burns asked me to look into what occurred and respond directly to you.

Thank you for your inquiry regarding renting a Ryder truck. Mr. Winkle, our trucks are not designed to transport livestock. Our moving vans are used primarily to move hardware items. I am sorry if we were not able to assist you in that area.

I have enclosed a discount coupon to be used on a future Ryder rental, if you need to move household items.

Thank you for your interest in Ryder.

Sincerely,

Patricia Marshall

Patricia Marshall
Customer Relations Specialist,
National Customer Service

Your File Number: 204342
cc: M.A. Burns
    J. Riordan

July 2, 1993

Mr. Mickey Owen
Baseball School
Department SN
Miller, MO 65707

Dear Mr. Owen:

My name is Wilber Winkle. I am 28 years old and I would like to attend your baseball
camp for kids December 26-31, 1993. I know I'll be much older than the rest of the
fellas, but coming to your camp is very important to me. Please hear my story.

I was raised by a mother who was a great lover of music. My summer vacations were
filled with piano and violin lessons. While all my buddies were playing baseball from
dawn to dusk, I was in my room getting yelled at for missing a note of "Moon River."
Tell me Mr. Owen, is that any way for a kid to grow up?

When I saw your ad in the *Sporting News,* I got goose bumps all over. I knew this was
my chance to put my childhood memories behind me and get on with my life. I need this,
Mr. Owen. Playing ball with the fellas for a week will enable me to enjoy the great game
of baseball I was unable to play as a boy. Although your ad says ages 8-19, I have very
little body hair and a few freckles. I'm sure the other kids won't catch on.

I tried the adult baseball camp, but it didn't help. I need to be with the kids, Mickey. I
just know you will understand. Enclosed is a $10 deposit for my enrollment in the camp.

Very truly yours,

Wilber Winkle
5764 Stevens Forest Rd. #606
Columbia, MD 21045

P. S. May I play shortstop?

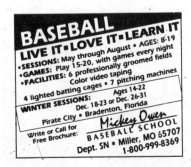

Mickey Owen

BASEBALL SCHOOL

July 12, 1993

Wilber Winkle
5764 Stevens Forest Road #606
Columbia, MD   21045

Dear Mr. Winkle:

Thank you for your interest in Mickey Owen Baseball School. We regret to inform you that we do not accept students over the age of 23.

We hope you continue your interest in baseball.

Sincerely,

Mickey Owen Baseball School
P.O. Box 88
Miller, MO   65707

July 17, 1993

Mr. Mickey Owen
Baseball School
Department SN
Miller, MO 65707

Dear Mickey:

It seems we've had a terrible misunderstanding. I made a mistake in my previous letter. I'm actually 23 years old, not 28. You made a mistake in your advertisement, when you said the school is for kids ages 8-19. In your letter, the truth came out -- you accept kids up to age 23. You were off by four years and I was off by five. Oh, well. I'm sure one day we'll look back at this and have a good laugh.

So now that we have this misunderstanding behind us, LET'S PLAY BALL!!! Please enroll me in the school. I have re-enclosed the check that you returned the first time. It's for $10 and it's my deposit. I really am 23 years old, although some say I look 28. I'd appreciate your letting me know what forms of identification I'll need to prove I'm 23. The funny thing is my license says I'm 28 also. It just goes to show you, Mickey, we're not the only ones who make these kinds of mistakes.

Thank you very much, Mick. I'll see you in December!!!

Very truly yours,

Wilber Winkle
5764 Stevens Forest Rd. #606
Columbia, MD 21045

P.S. I'll play any position you want except first base.

BASEBALL SCHOOL

10-19-93

Wilber Winkle
5764 Stevens Forest Rd., Apt. 606
Columbia, MD 21045-3645

Dear Mr. Winkle

We do not accept anyone over the age of 22 for either the winter
school or the summer school. We cannot accept your application
because you are over the age that can attend the school.

I am sending back your check for $10.00.

Sincerely,

Brandy Garrett
Brandy Garrett

August 23, 1993

Mr. Mickey Owen
Baseball School
Department SN
Miller, MO 65707

Dear Mickey,

This is turning into a real comedy of errors. I recently received my check back from your school, yet there was no explanation. The check was the only thing in the envelope. I assume it was just a sloppy mistake. Please don't come down too hard on the clerical department. Anyway, I've enclosed the check once again so you may credit my account accordingly.

My friend who wrote the check, John Homans, said you called him and left a message on his answering machine requesting references for me. I never realized I would need references for a baseball camp, but I guess you want to make sure you don't get a lot of scrubs out there. The only problem is that John Homans has never seen me play ball, so he really can't assure you that I'm a half-decent ballplayer. Please let me know how many references I'll need to attend the camp. I'll be glad to send you as many as you need.

Since December is now only four month away, I figure it's high time to purchase my airline tickets. The fares are really low now and the tickets are much cheaper to buy in advance.

Mickey, I must admit that my game is really coming around. I've been going to the batting cage every day to work on my swing. At camp, do you have an MVP for the week? If so, I think I'm going to be the odds-on favorite.

Thanks again, Mick. See you soon!

Very truly yours,

Wilber Winkle
5764 Stevens Forest Rd. #606
Columbia, MD 21045

November 13, 1993

Mr. Mickey Owen
Baseball School
Department SN
Miller, MO 65707

Dear Mickey:

I'm very disappointed with you and everyone associated with your baseball camp. It's becoming perfectly clear that you don't want me to attend. Someone even changed the rules so I would not qualify. Your letter of 7/12/93 says "we do not accept students over the age of 23." As soon as you learned I was 23, the rules changed to 22. What gives, Mickey? Why is there a conspiracy against my playing ball at the camp?

I think I'm at least entitled to an explanation as to why I'm not welcome there. I wonder if it's even legal to deny a qualifying applicant based on age, especially considering I met the qualifications when I applied. Don't worry, I'm not the type who will sue. I couldn't live with myself knowing I brought trouble to an organization dedicated to giving kids the opportunity to play ball.

I'm tired of fighting, Mick. You've hit me with a left hook and knocked me to the canvas. I realize you don't want me there and I'll reluctantly give up my dream of playing ball at your camp. Please accept my generous donation of $23 to the camp in the hopes that other kids will not have to endure the suffering I have experienced.

Very truly yours,

Wilber Winkle
5764 Stevens Forest Rd. #606
Columbia, MD 21045

January 26, 1994

Mr. Mickey Owen
Baseball School
Department SN
Miller, MO 65707

Dear Mick,

Just wanted to verify that you received my generous donation of $23 for the baseball camp. I usually get a thank-you note or acknowledgment when I make contributions of this kind. I'm somewhat surprised I haven't heard from you yet.

If it wouldn't be too much trouble, please send me a receipt for my donation. I deduct these "gifts" on my taxes and you never know when Uncle Sam will come around for an audit. I would also like to know how my contribution was spent.

Take care, Mickey. If you raise the age limits for next year, be sure to let me know. I'll stay in tip-top shape just in case.

Very truly yours,

Wilber Winkle

Wilber Winkle
5764 Stevens Forest Rd. #606
Columbia, MD 21045

February 26, 1997

Mr. Mickey Owen
Baseball School
Department SN
Miller, MO 65707

Dear Mickey,

How have you been? I know it's been a few years since I've written, but I just had to share some wonderful news with you! Are you ready? I recently moved to Florida and now live just minutes away from the ball fields in Bradenton where you conduct your camps! Isn't that fantastic?!

Please let me know if you have increased the age limits since you last wrote. I figure that even if I'm a little older than the rest of the guys, you might let me "slide" (get it?) with a wink and a nod since I live so close to the camp. If you still won't let me play, perhaps I can pitch batting practice or sweep the infield between innings. Heck, I'll even do the laundry as long as you let me hang around with you and the other fellas.

I know things got a little heated between us a few years ago, but I'm a firm believer that time heals all wounds. What do you say we let bygones be bygones, put our differences aside, and PLAY BALL?!

Can't wait to hear back from you, Mick. Don't forget to let me know the age eligibility requirements.

Very truly yours,

Wilber Winkle
PO Box 434
Mango, FL 33550

August 1, 1996

Cunard Cruise Lines
Customer Relations
555 5th Avenue
New York, NY 10017

Dear Sirs:

Is it mandatory to use silverware during meals on your cruises? I've grown quite accustomed to using my hands while eating and I want to know if this will be a problem. The only time things get a little messy for me is when I eat pasta dishes and several desserts, such as ice cream and pudding. For the sake of the other passengers, I'll try to avoid these dishes if at all possible.

Thank you for your assistance.

Very truly yours,

Wilber Winkle
5764 Stevens Forest Rd. #606
Columbia, MD 21045

CUNARD

August 16, 1996

Mr. Wilber Winkle
5764 Stevens Forest Rd. #606
Columbia, MD 21045

Dear Mr. Winkle:

This will refer to your recent correspondence.

Thank you for taking the time to contact us and for providing the opportunity to address your concerns directly. Upon receipt of your letter, I immediately contacted the Hotel Manager on board our flagship and herein communicate his response to your query. Kindly be advised that our on board staff is sensitive to the needs and requests of all our guests; as such, they would be happy to serve all your meals in your selected cabin accommodations during your stay on board ship.

Once again, thank you for your interest in Cunard Line Ltd., and for the time you have expended in writing to us. It is always our pleasure to serve you.

Sincerely,

Gladys Maldonado
Customer Affairs

Tabloid proclaims 12 senators are space aliens

Associated Press

WASHINGTON — Going where no congressional critics have gone before, a supermarket tabloid contends that 12 U.S. senators are space aliens. And many of them are "admitting" their otherworldly origins.

"At last the cat is out of the bag, although this isn't exactly the way I intended to tell my family and friends," Sen. Bennett Johnston, D-La., told the *Weekly World News* newspaper for an article in its June 7 issue.

"It's all true," it quotes Sen. Phil Gramm, R-Texas, as saying. "I'm amazed that it's taken you so long to find out."

Yesterday, spokesmen for both senators confirmed the quotes given to the newspaper, which was open about its intentions when it contacted Senate offices several months ago.

"They called us up and said, 'This is real tongue-in-cheek and we're doing this for fun," said Tom McMahon, spokesman for another alleged alien, Sen. Howell Heflin, D-Ala.

Others named as space aliens are Sens. William Cohen, R-Maine; Dennis DeConcini, D-Ariz.; Christopher Dodd, D-Conn.; Jay Rockefeller, D-W.Va.; John Glenn, D-Ohio; Orrin Hatch, R-Utah; Nancy Kassebaum, R-Kan.; Sam Nunn, D-Ga.; and Alan Simpson, R-Wyo. The final five "came out of the alien closet two years ago," the paper quotes author and UFO specialist Nathaniel Dean as saying.

But Simpson spokesman Charles Pelkey remained mysterious about his boss' status.

"We've got only one thing to say: Klattu Barado Nikto," Mr. Pelkey said.

That was an alien code from "The Day the Earth Stood Still," a 1951 science fiction movie about a robot-aided alien who lands in Washington and warns of the dangers of war.

Gramm spokesman Larry Neal asked where in the universe the senator is from, cracked, "It's Remulak in our case. I don't know where the other guys are from."

Recognizing that Mr. Gramm's alien status could impede his presidential aspirations since American presidents must be natural-born U.S. citizens, Mr. Neal later backtracked, saying Mr. Gramm was born here but his parents came from Remulak.

Two years ago, when Ms. Kassebaum humorously confirmed her "alien" status, "we got phone calls and letters from people who were terribly upset by it, and in fact believed there was some truth to the reports," said spokesman Mike Horak. "You'd never think that people take this seriously."

ASSOCIATED PRESS

The cover of the June 7 edition of the Weekly World News.

October 15, 1994

The Honorable Senator Phil Gramm
The Russell Office Bldg.
Room SR-370
Washington, DC 20510

Dear Senator Gramm,

I was pleased to read in the "Weekly World News" that you finally came out of the closet and admitted that your parents are from the planet Remulak. I know it took great courage to do this. Frankly, I think this country needs some leadership from other worlds to turn things around. Perhaps you and the eleven other aliens in Congress can prevent us from making some of the mistakes your ancestors made.

I'm a bit puzzled that your revelation didn't get more press. I guess it all stems from the fact that, like the Roswell incident, the government and press do not think the American public can deal with it. And speaking of the Roswell incident, were the aliens killed in the crash from your planet? I certainly hope not.

Please let me know how many other Senators are from your planet. Also, any plans to go back?

I understand you have presidential aspirations. I'm willing to do anything to help with the campaign. Your Remulakin background may pose some problems, but nothing you can't overcome. After all, we earthlings have made quite a mess for ourselves. You have a strong argument for real change. In fact, I've got a good campaign slogan for you, "End the gridlock, vote Remulakin."

I look forward to hearing back, as I'm anxious to know what I can do for you in your campaign for President (aside from offering advice).

Very truly yours,

Wilber Winkle

Wilber Winkle
5764 Stevens Forest Rd. #606
Columbia, MD 21045

February 28, 1995

The Honorable Phil Gramm
The Russell Office Bldg.
Room SR-370
Washington DC 20510

Dear Senator Gramm:

I'm a bit disappointed you have not responded to my earlier letter. I guess you've been busy getting your Presidential campaign underway. I think you've got a shot at it, but stop putting yourself down and saying things like, "I don't know if Americans are ready to elect an ugly man like myself." You ain't ugly, Senator. You may resemble a turtle the way your head sticks out, but turtles are kinda cute in my opinion. I suppose Remulak has an atmosphere similar to Earth's, because, aside from your turtle features, you look almost human!

I saw your press conference when you announced your candidacy for President. I'm still confused that no mention was made of your Remulakin background. I also read a profile of you and your lovely wife in my local paper, but again no mention of Remulak. What's the scoop, Senator? There's no use trying to keep it hidden. Better let the American people know now about your heritage rather than waiting until election time. If you don't, I'm sure that grouch Bob Dole will leak it to the press right when it will hurt you the most. I think we Americans are ready for a "different" type of candidate, but you must give us a little time to absorb it all. I strongly urge you to release this information at once. Why not do it on the Brinkley show this Sunday?

Again, please let me know how I can support you in your quest for the Presidency. I am also willing to work on "damage control" after you finally come clean on your heritage. I look forward to hearing from you soon.

Very truly yours,

Wilber Winkle
5764 Stevens Forest Rd. #606
Columbia, MD 21045

March 8, 1996

Mr. Wilber Winkle
5764 Stevens Forest Rd
Columbia, MD 21045

Dear Wilber:

Ending my campaign for President was one of the toughest things I have ever had to do, but I wanted you to know that even as I was withdrawing, I knew that it had been one of the great privileges of my life to have spent a year in the company of people like you, fighting for the ideals that we believe in.

Those of us who fought in this effort should remember the words of Henry V to his bedraggled army as they prepared to meet the vastly superior forces of France: "He that outlives this day and comes safe home will stand a tip-toe when this day is named . . . Gentlemen in England now a-bed shall think themselves accursed they were not here, and hold their manhood cheap while any speaks that fought with us . . ."

Today, I have a deeper love and a more profound respect for my country and my countrymen than ever before. Thank you for answering my call and for being ready to stake your time, your talent, your money and, most importantly, your reputation on me. I came away from this race humbled, not by the loss, but by the fact that you chose to stand beside me. I will never forget your help and friendship.

I'm back on the job in the Senate, working hard for the things we believe in: less government and more freedom, balancing the budget, reforming welfare, grabbing criminals by the throat. I know that sooner or later, America will have to face up to the choice between unlimited government and unlimited opportunity, and when that day comes, I intend to be there, ready to lead.

I'm up for re-election to the Senate in Texas, and I plan to wage a vigorous re-election campaign.

I leave this race with the firm conviction that no defeat is final. Please stay in touch with me and count on the fact that I will stay in touch with you.

Thank you for your help and friendship, and thank you for believing in me.

Yours respectfully,

Phil

PHIL GRAMM
United States Senator
Texas

P.O. BOX 33119 • WASHINGTON, D.C. 20033 • 202-467-8600 • FAX 202-467-8693
P.O. BOX 8300 • LB 553 • DALLAS, TEXAS 75205 • 214-360-3700 • FAX 214-360-0589
email info@gramm96.org
PAID FOR BY PHIL GRAMM FOR PRESIDENT, INC.

December 11, 1993

JEOPARDY
1040 North Las Palmas
Hollywood, CA 90038

HI GUYS!

I thoroughly enjoyed the tournaments that aired last month. "Celebrity Jeopardy" was a lot of fun, the "Tournament of Champions" was as exciting as ever, and the "10th Anniversary Tournament" was really a keen idea. It was great seeing the champions of yesteryear return for more competition.

Since these tournaments appear to be very popular, I have a great idea I want to tell you about. The most humiliating part of a show is when a contestant finishes in the hole and is not able to participate in "Final Jeopardy." Although we never see it at home, it must be a humiliating experience to be ushered off the stage and not even be able to shake Alec's hand at the end of the show.

Couldn't these poor saps at least play "Final Jeopardy" for fun? Why the rush to get rid of them? What's worse is the fact that they actually have to pay the show all the money they lose!

I propose a "Tournament of Losers" competition. Bring back all the losers from the previous season and give them a chance to redeem themselves in front of a national audience. And if they finish in the hole again, bring them back the next season as two-time losers! A "Two Time Loser" tournament would surely get huge ratings! Americans always like rooting for the underdog.

I'm not looking to be compensated in any way for this idea, but would like Alec to give me credit at the beginning of the tournament. Please let me know the dates it'll air so I can tell all my friends that my name will be mentioned.

Very truly yours,

Wilber Winkle
5764 Stevens Forest Road #606
Columbia, MD 21045

JEOPARDY!

December 21, 1993

Wilber Winkle
5764 Stevens Forest Road, #606
Columbia, MD   21045

Dear Wilber:

Thank you for your recent letter and comments regarding our
Jeopardy! program. I am always delighted to hear from
viewers, especially when they write with suggestions.

Although we have considered the idea of bringing back
"nonwinning" contestants, at the present time, we have no
plans to do so. However, we might change this at some
point in the future. Meanwhile, I hope that you will
continue to watch and enjoy our show.

Yours sincerely,

Alex Trebek
Host/JEOPARDY!

1040

North

Las Palmas

Hollywood,

California

90038

Tel:

213 466 4487

MERV GRIFFIN ENTERPRISES a SONY PICTURES ENTERTAINMENT company

July 14, 1993

The Honorable Thomas Foley
Speaker of the House
1201 Longworth House Office Building
Washington, DC 20510

Dear Speaker Foley,

Just wanted to congratulate you on doing a great job as Speaker of the House. I watch C-Span about eleven hours a day. Needless to say, I see you so often that I feel like we're close friends.

On Saturday, May 29, 1993, I took a plane to Barbados for a vacation with my girlfriend. Her name is Luci and she's very nice. When exiting the plane, I was flabbergasted to see you walk right past me. I tried to catch up with you on the tarmac, but a bunch of guys in suits came and took you away. Was that really you? It was awful hot down there and I could have been hallucinating.

Also, the man I saw leaving the plane was carrying a black bag with the MTV emblem on the side. Are you a rock music fan? If so, who's your favorite group? I also want to know where you got the bag, as I would like to obtain one just like it. If the bag is good enough for you, then it must be good enough for me.

I know your schedule is busy, but please take time to respond and let me know if that was really you in Barbados. I told all my friends I saw you but they don't believe me.

Very truly yours,

Wilber Winkle

Wilber Winkle
5764 Stevens Forest Rd. #606
Columbia, MD 21045

November 1, 1993

The Honorable Thomas Foley
Speaker of the House
1201 Longworth House Office Building
Washington, DC 20510

Dear Mr. Speaker:

As summer has turned to fall and the leaves have changed their colors, my mind still takes me back to that wonderful summer day in Barbados. There you were, gorgeous gray hair blowing in the breeze, walking confidently on the tarmac.

Unfortunately, the passing of time has made me less sure that it really *was* you. My friends now mock me for making my slight claim to fame. And they say your refusal to respond to my first letter indicates it must have been a case of mistaken identity. I tell them you're a busy man and that you'll write as soon as you can. But it hurts to hear them snicker.

Although I have my doubts, I still believe in my heart that it *was* you in Barbados. Please let me know one way or the other. I can take it.

And if it was you, please explain the mystery of the MTV bag.

Whatever you say, you're the greatest!

Very truly yours,

Wilber Winkle
5764 Stevens Forest Rd. #606
Columbia, MD 21045

November 12, 1993

Mr. Wilber Winkle
5764 Stevens Forest Road, #606
Columbia, MD 21045

Dear Mr. Winkle:

   Thank you for your recent letter indicating that you saw me
on my last trip to Barbados. It is not often that I can get away
for vacation and you may have seen me during that time.

   In answer to your question regarding the type of music I
enjoy, I enjoy all music and fortunately have a great selection
to choose from. Thanks for taking the time to write.

   With very best wishes.

                    Sincerely,

                    Thomas S. Foley
                    Member of Congress

TSF:tt

June 12, 1996

Jeff Perlee, Director
New York Lottery
P.O. Box 7500
Schenectady, NY 12301-7500

Dear Mr. Perlee:

I'm going to win the Lotto drawing on July 17, 1996. For the past two years, I painstakingly analyzed the bouncing Ping-Pong balls and have now conclusively determined which balls will be sucked into the tube on the above-mentioned date. My extensive study included analysis of past winning numbers, and I'm happy to say that the fruits of my labor will soon be realized. While I certainly won't reveal *now* all of the winning numbers for July 17, rest assured that one of them will be 37.

You can expect to see me in your office at 9:45 A.M. on Thursday, July 18, to collect my prize. I wish to remain anonymous, so please call off the media hounds. Since it is very important that my winning remain a secret, I foresee a bit of a problem escaping Lottery Headquarters with my prize. I've seen preceding winners on TV. The checks they hold up look like they're at least eight feet wide! Do you think it's possible to leave with such a check and not be seen? Please let me know if you have any secret tunnels or back entrances that will make it easier for me.

In order to thank you for your anticipated cooperation, I thought I would make your own wallet a little heavier. The winning Pick-3 combination on July 10th will be 6-9-4. If you're not allowed to play the game yourself, please give these numbers to a friend or relative who's currently strapped for cash.

Thank you very much for your help.

Very truly yours,

Wilber Winkle
5764 Stevens Forest Road #606
Columbia, MD 21045

January 5, 1997

Jeff Perlee, Director
New York Lottery
PO Box 7500
Schenectady, NY 12301-7500

Dear Mr. Perlee:

I'm disappointed that you didn't respond to my letter of June 12, 1996. If you weren't able to keep my winning a secret, I just wish you would have taken a minute to let me know instead of leaving me hanging. Because it was obvious that I was not going to gain your cooperation, I decided not to play the game on July 17, 1996. I have continued my research, however, and my new calculations show which numbers will hit on February 15, 1997. I am asking once again for your assistance, as I would rather not play at all if my anonymity cannot not be guaranteed when collecting the prize.

I have moved to Florida since my last letter, but thanks to my satellite dish, my analysis of the New York Lottery Ping-Pong balls continues. I also have friends in New York who stand ready to purchase my tickets for me once I hear back from you, so please don't delay. If you will not cooperate, I'll have to pick another state and begin my research all over again. Considering the fact that it took three long years to figure out the New York system, I'm sure you can understand my reluctance to start from scratch with another state lottery. I would hate for all this work to go down the tubes for nothing, so please respond ASAP.

And one other thing: I sincerely apologize for giving you the wrong Pick-3 numbers for the July 10th drawing. I missed because I forgot that there were only 30 days in June, instead of 31. By adding in that extra day, my calculations were thrown completely out of whack. I'm really sorry for the mistake and am enclosing a dollar to reimburse whomever forked over a buck for the ticket.

I eagerly anticipate your reply. I hope to meet you in person on February 16th.

Very truly yours,

Wilber Winkle
P.O. Box 434
Mango, FL 33550

141

Jeff Perlee, Director

February 5, 1997

Wilber Winkle
P.O. Box 434
Mango, FL 33550

Dear Mr. Winkle:

Thank you for your recent letter regarding the New York Lottery. I appreciate your comments.

Your theory that there is a "system" that can predict winning lottery numbers is erroneous. Drawings are conducted under carefully controlled conditions that produce unpredictable, random results. Even the equipment used in the drawing process is changed at random intervals to assure that any variations in the equipment are canceled out by the impossibility of predicting which set of numbered balls will be used in which drawing machine for a particular drawing. For the same reason, ball sets are regularly weighed and measured and periodically replaced.

It would be impossible for you to collect any New York Lottery prize greater than $600 without having your identity available to the public. Lottery prize funds are public money, and the public has every right to know the identities of prize winners. The Lottery customarily announces the name of every large prize winner, together with the name of the municipality in which the winner resides. The Lottery does not, however, release the street addresses or telephone numbers of prize winners.

Additionally, any material requested from the Lottery must be paid with a money order. Since you did not enclose a money order with a request for materials, we are therefore returning your $1.00 bill.

If there is any additional information I can provide, please don't hesitate to call.

Sincerely,

Richard A. Grenell
Press Secretary

RAG/ssmw

July 29, 1996

Coalition of Drug-Free Horse Racing
1000 29th St. NW, Suite T100
Washington DC 20007

Dear Sirs:

Just wanted to drop you a quick note to congratulate your organization on the fine efforts being put forth to clean up the horse racing industry. It's sad to think that our four-legged friends are not immune from the drug epidemic sweeping the land. I imagine that race horses must be particularly vulnerable due to the industry they work in. Because of the difficulty of coping with success achieved on the track, they all too frequently turn to drugs to ease their fears and anxieties.

Rather than concentrating strictly on the addicts themselves, why not focus on the suppliers? Let's be realistic about the situation. Horses would have a tough time obtaining and using most drugs without human intervention. In fact, I fail to see how horses alone could obtain many of the potent drugs currently in circulation, such as crack and heroin. I recommend around-the-clock surveillance of *all* stables so we can determine exactly what's going on after the barn doors are closed for the evening.

I also recommend a firm anti-drug policy in the racing industry. Any horse that tests positive for drugs should be banned for life! I haven't heard of any suspensions in the racing industry lately, and I strongly suspect that the current drug policy is too lenient.

Also, why not ban the drug users from stud farms as well? Half of them would rather be on these farms than race, so where's the incentive for good behavior? Let's make the stud farm a reward for a fine career rather than a haven for down and out addicts.

Please let me know how I personally can help to eliminate drugs from the racing industry. I've got plenty of free time on my hands, so perhaps you would like me to go to Pimlico and check things out.

I look forward to hearing from you.

Very truly yours,

Wilber Winkle

Wilber Winkle
5764 Stevens Forest Rd. #606
Columbia, MD 21045

143

AMERICAN HORSE PROTECTION ASSOCIATION, INC.
1000 - 29th Street, N.W., Suite T-100, Washington, D.C. 20007
(202) 965-0500

A NATIONAL NON-PROFIT ORGANIZATION
DEDICATED SOLELY TO THE WELFARE OF HORSES,
BOTH WILD AND DOMESTIC

August 8, 1996

Mr. Wilber Winkle
5764 Stevens Forest Road #606
Columbia, MD 21045

Dear Mr. Winkle:

Thank you for contacting the American Horse Protection Association. For more information concerning drugs within the racing industry, we recommend you contact: The Jockey Club, 40 E. 52nd Street, New York, NY 10022; Thoroughbred Racing Protective Bureau, 420 Fair Hill Drive, #2, Elkton, MD 21921; Horsemen's Benevolent & Protective Association at (305) 935-4700.

AHPA is a national non-profit humane organization devoted exclusively to equine welfare. Since 1966, the Association and its members have worked to promote responsible horse ownership, the humane treatment of horses in competition, the humane transportation of equines, and the preservation of America's wild horses and burros.

The Association provides information on proper horse care, hosts educational seminars and events, and works to improve federal, state and local laws affecting equines and ensure that existing law is effectively enforced. AHPA works with humane officers, community officials, individuals, and other organizations to protect equines from abuse and neglect.

Our membership is quite diverse and includes horse owners, horse enthusiasts, horse clubs, and humane organizations from around the country. Much of our success lies with the dedication of our members and volunteers.

If you should have any further questions, please do not hesitate to contact us again. Thank you again for your interest in AHPA.

Sincerely,

Amy E. Ciok
Administrative Assistant

Enclosures

144

June 2, 1995

Kellogg's Company
Arnold G. Langbo, CEO
One Kellogg Square
Battle Creek, MI 49016

Dear Mr. Langbo:

I have one quick question regarding "Frosted Flakes." What should go in the bowl first, the cereal or the milk? A friend of mine saw me pouring the cereal into the bowl first and called me a jackass. He said the milk should go first in order to keep the flakes from getting soggy.

Please let me know what the correct procedure is. I don't take too kindly to being called a jackass and I'd greatly appreciate a letter from you saying that I'm right in pouring the cereal first.

Very truly yours,

Wilber Winkle
5764 Stevens Forest Rd. #606
Columbia, MD 21045

June 23, 1995

Mr. Wilber Winkle
#606
5764 Stevens Forest Rd.
Columbia, MD 21045

Dear Mr. Winkle:

Thank you for your recent letter to Arnold Langbo, which was directed
to Consumer Affairs for response. We appreciate your interest in our
products.

To be perfectly frank, I don't believe there is any hard and fast rule
pertaining to which goes in the bowl first, the cereal or the milk. I
will say, however, that it is usually pretty hard to add cereal to a
bowl full of milk without having the cereal spill out all over the
table, so I'm siding with you in this case!

In any event, we usually recommend that you proceed to eat the cereal
right after you have combined the milk and the cereal to ensure that it
stays crispy nearly to the end of the bowl.

Thank you again for writing, and I hope this helps you with the problem
you encountered with your friend.

Sincerely,

Diane Backus

Dianne L. Backus
Consumer Specialist
Consumer Affairs Department

dlb/cl

1278452A

Kellogg Company / Corporate Headquarters
One Kellogg Square / P.O. Box 3599 / Battle Creek, Michigan 49016-3599 (616) 961-2000

February 4, 1994

M&M - MARS
Division of MARS, INC.
Attention: <u>Consumer Relations</u>
Hackettstown, NJ 07840

Dear Sirs:

Something has been bothering me for over 20 years and I would like to finally get it off my chest. I eat approximately three packs of plain M&Ms a week. Over the course of 20 years, I've eaten 3,120 packs. In every single pack I've eaten, there have been more brown M&Ms than any other color, though one time there was a tie, with 16 browns and 16 greens. In every other pack, it's hardly ever close, with the brown ones often twice the total of their nearest competitor.

Just to show you I'm not making this up, I bought a pack today and here are the results:

Brown	23
Tan	11
Orange	8
Red	5
Yellow	5
Green	5

Why must the brown ones dominate every pack? I have some theories of my own:

1. Brown ones are cheaper to make because not as much artificial coloring is needed. Chocolate is naturally brown;
2. Green and red ones are made in the same numbers, but have to be saved for the Christmas season; and
3. People generally prefer the taste of the brown ones.

I bought some Peanut M&Ms to see if the results would be the same. Apparently the brown ones don't dominate in the Peanuts as they do in the Plains.

Green	6
Orange	5
Brown	5
Yellow	4
Red	2

I was also surprised that, while the tan ones finished a respectable second in the Plains, they were completely unrepresented in the Peanuts. In fact, I don't believe I've <u>ever</u> seen a tan Peanut M&M. Why is this the case?

Please shed some light on these mysteries. I await your response with much anticipation.

Very truly yours,

Wilber Winkle
5764 Stevens Forest Road #606
Columbia, MD 21045

a division of Mars, Incorporated

High Street, Hackettstown, New Jersey 07840 • Telephone 908-852-1000

March 10, 1994

Mr. Wilber Winkle
5764 Stevens Forest Road #606
Columbia, MD 21045

Dear Mr. Winkle:

Thank you so much for your inquiry about "M&M's"® Chocolate Candies.

Our color blends were selected by conducting consumer preference tests, which indicate the assortment of colors that pleased the greatest number of people and created the most attractive overall effect. The color ratio for "M&M's"® Plain Chocolate Candies is 30% brown, 20% yellow, 20% red, 10% orange, 10% green and 10% tan. Brown is the predominant color because it is indicative of chocolate. "M&M's"® Peanut Chocolate Candies are currently produced in five colors -- 20% each of brown, yellow, green, red and orange. All colors are certified pure food colors approved by the FDA.

Each large production batch is blended precisely to those ratios and mixed thoroughly. However, since the individual packages are filled by weight on high-speed equipment, and not by count, it is possible to occasionally have an unusual color distribution.

At the present time, our Marketing Staff is not anticipating adding any other new colors.

Because of the difference in the sizes of the individual candies there is a variation of pieces per package. However, the package should be the indicated weight.

Your interest is appreciated. We hope you will continue to enjoy M&M/MARS products and remain our valued consumer.

Sincerely,

Kathy Ljungquist
Kathy Ljungquist
Consumer Affairs

KML/bww 0272771A
Enclosures

OFFICIAL SNACK FOOD SPONSOR   OF THE 1994 WORLD CUP

October 9, 1994

Kathy Ljungquist
Consumer Affairs
M&M/MARS
High Street
Hackettstown, NJ 07840

Dear Kathy:

Hope you're doing well. I've had a great summer and I'm gearing up for the winter. In the summer, I like to freeze M&Ms so they don't melt in my hand. I must admit, though, that it's kind of neat when, on a hot summer day, you pour a bunch of M&Ms into your hand and it turns all different colors from the melting candy.

In your correspondence of March 10, 1994, you stated that the Marketing Staff was not anticipating the addition of any new colors. Is this still the case? I have a really keen suggestion that I trust you will pass on to the appropriate personnel. How about blue M&Ms? I think they would please a great number of people and create the most attractive overall effect. Since browns account for 30 percent of all Plains now, you could drop them to 25% and start blue along slowly at 5%. Brown would still be the dominant color, and the new color of blue would be a fantastic and exciting addition.

I should tell you, in case you don't already know, that some of the Jordan Almonds you buy at the movies are blue, and that color mixture seems to go over pretty well, at least according to some friends I've talked to.

Please find enclosed a $10 donation. Please forward it to the Marketing Department to help with the additional consumer tests needed for the blue M&Ms. Better yet, why not cash it in for a nice dinner for yourself as a reward for how nice you've been to me (I won't tell anybody)?

Also enclosed are letters I received from Congressman Joe Skeen and Senator Conrad Burns. Both are M&M lovers and I thought perhaps you'd consider them for some commercials or something.

Thanks for everything, Kathy. I can't wait to hear back from you with regard to my ideas about blue M&Ms. Enjoy the dinner!!

Very truly yours,

Wilber Winkle
5764 Stevens Forest Rd. #606
Columbia, MD 21045

149

a division of Mars, Incorporated
High Street, Hackettstown, New Jersey 07840 ● Telephone 908-852-1000

October 14, 1994

Mr. Wilber Winkle
5764 Stevens Forest Road #606
Columbia, MD 21045

Dear Mr. Winkle:

Thank you for your most recent letter regarding "M&M's"® Chocolate
Candies.

Our Research Department conduct consumer preference tests from time to
time to determine which color assortments please the greatest number of
people.

Although blue is generally not associated with food and not used in our
blend, "M&M's"® Brand HOLIDAYS Chocolate Candies contain a light blue
in the pastel assortment available in the spring. We have also had
dark blue in other Holiday assortments in the past.

I am returning the money order as you may want to use it.

Your interest is appreciated. Please accept the enclosed store coupon
for a treat with the compliments of M&M/MARS.

Sincerely,

Kathy Ljungquist

Kathy Ljungquist
Consumer Affairs

KML/cl 0272771B

OFFICIAL SNACK FOOD SPONSOR   OF THE 1994 WORLD CUP

M&M's considering a seventh color for its candy mix

Associated Press

Just in case some M&M's melt in your hand, not in your mouth, the manufacturer at least wants you to like the color.

M&M-Mars is asking fans of the candy-coated chocolate pieces to select the newest hue for the mix. Don't get too wild, though — the choices for Color No. 7 are blue, purple and pink.

Candy-lovers also may vote to leave the mix as it is: brown, yellow, orange, red, green and tan.

M&M-Mars is considering a seventh color so its candy reflects new color preferences of the 1990s, said Pat D'Amato, a spokeswoman for the company, based in Hackettstown, N.J.

M&M's, introduced in 1940, are made in different-hued mixes four times a year: Christmas, Valentine's Day, Halloween and Easter.

The traditional mix has remained unchanged since 1949 — except for the decade-long absence of the red piece. Red was removed over a scare about food dye and restored in 1987.

Ballots to vote on the new color are available at most stores that sell candy. The results will be announced April 18.

If voters go for a change the new M&M's should be in stores by September, Ms. D'Amato said.

To drum up interest, people dressed as pink, purple and blue M&M's will make an appearance at the Super Bowl and dance at Mardi Gras.

"I think they ought to leave it the way it is," Maryann Mandonia of Pittsburgh said as she shopped at a Newark (N.J.) International Airport newsstand. She didn't like the new choices "because they are medicine colors."

But Leslie Vasquez, a cashier at the newsstand, said she would like to see a purple M&M.

"It's a nice color, and I think that people are going to like it," she said.

March 7, 1995

Kathy Ljungquist
Consumer Affairs, M&M/MARS
High Street
Hackettstown, NJ 07840

Dear Kathy:

I was glad to read recently that your company has finally decided to add blue M&Ms to the usual Plains assortment (see the attached article from the Associated Press). I'm a bit disappointed, however, at your planned promotional activities. In my opinion, having people dress up as M&Ms at the Super Bowl, or getting them to dance in costume at Mardi Gras is absolutely ridiculous.

As for the company's scheduled contest, it doesn't take a rocket scientist to figure out that "Blue" will be the runaway winner. Just look at the weak competition you've lined up. Even running "Pink" as a candidate is a joke. No self-respecting man will ever vote for it. So, if the voters are evenly split between the sexes, "Pink" will start out with a 50 percent disapproval rating (unless some men vote for it), and anyone who knows anything about campaigns will tell you that it's impossible to get elected with negatives that high.

As for "Purple," you'd have to be demented to vote for such a ridiculous color. And, if it somehow managed to win, I can see the folks at "Good-N-Plenty" splapping a lawsuit on your company so fast it'd make your head spin. Purple "Good-N-Plenty" has been around for years. You just can't go out and copy them.

Here's my prediction for the election's final results:
BLUE   *30%*
No Changes   *27%*
Pink   *23%*
Purple   *20%*

Curiously, Peanut M&Ms were not mentioned in the story about the color contest. Will "Blue" be added to the peanut variety as well? Also, are you going to take my suggestion and start "Blue" at 5% of the whole pack? I personally think you should take away a little from each existing color, but leave "Brown" alone. In any event, it's critical for "Brown" to be in the 25-30 percent range and remain the dominant color. With anything less, one would lose the sense of eating chocolate, and that could be catastrophic to M&M's reputation. Kathy, I hope to get an election update from you soon. Go "Blue"!!!

Very truly yours,

Wilber Winkle
5764 Stevens Forest Road, #606
Columbia, MD 21045

December 13, 1995

Consumer Affairs
Attn: Kathy Ljungquist
M&M/MARS
High Street
Hackettstown, NJ 07840

Dear Kathy:

We've been corresponding for quite some time now, and I would be remiss if I didn't wish you and yours a very joyous holiday season.

If you recall, I'm the one who came up with the idea of adding the "blue" color to Plain M&Ms. You wrote me back and said you didn't like the idea, but your company went ahead and started an election process to nominate "Blue" anyway. Some of my friends say your company probably liked my idea right away, but staged the election so it wouldn't look like you got it from me. Everyone knew "Blue" was gonna win, so why bother with the charade?

My friends also tell me that I'm due some money for thinking up the idea, and that you just don't want to pay me. I'm not looking for money, Kathy, but it would be nice to get a letter thanking me for my contribution. That way I could show my family at Christmas what I've accomplished. Some of my relatives like to call me a jackass, and I would really like to get them to stop. Perhaps when they realize that the blue M&M was my brainchild, they'll stop calling me names.

I've enclosed some of my letters from the past to prove that it really was my idea to add the blue color. I'm sure the final decision was made by some Manager, but I feel I should at least get some credit for planting the seed. Don't you agree?

Thanks again, Kathy. Please get the thank-you letter out to me as soon as possible so I can get it in time for Christmas.

Very truly yours,

Wilber Winkle
5764 Stevens Forest Rd. #606
Columbia, MD 21045

FITZPATRICK, CELLA, HARPER & SCINTO
277 PARK AVENUE
NEW YORK 10172-0194
212-758-2400
FACSIMILE (212) 758-2982

JOSEPH M. FITZPATRICK
LAWRENCE F. SCINTO
WILLIAM J. BRUNET
ROBERT L. BAECHTOLD
JOHN A. O'BRIEN
JOHN A. KRAUSE
HENRY J. RENK
DAVID F. RYAN
PETER SAXON
ANTHONY M. ZUPCIC
CHARLES P. BAKER
STEVAN J. BOSSES
EDWARD E. VASSALLO
RONALD A. CLAYTON
NICHOLAS M. CANNELLA
HUGH C. BARRETT
DAVID M. QUINLAN
PASQUALE A. RAZZANO
JOHN W. BEHRINGER *
LAWRENCE A. STAHL

LEONARD P. DIANA
WILLIAM M. WANNISKY *
NINA SHREVE
ROBERT H. FISCHER
DONALD J. CURRY
WARREN E. OLSEN *
NICHOLAS N. KALLAS
BRUCE C. HAAS
ABIGAIL F. COUSINS
THOMAS H. BECK
LAWRENCE S. PERRY
MICHAEL K. O'NEILL
RICHARD P. BAUER *
ERROL B. TAYLOR
NICHOLAS GROOMBRIDGE
LESLIE K. MITCHELL
SCOTT K. REED
FREDRICK M. ZULLOW
SCOTT D. MALPEDE *
THOMAS J. O'CONNELL *

LAURA A. BAUER
CHRISTOPHER P. WRIST
GARY M. JACOBS *
STEVEN E. WARNER *
VICTOR J. GERACI
MARYANNE DICKEY
PENINA WOLLMAN
STEVEN C. KLINE
DAVID L. SCHAEFFER
JACK CUBERT *
MARK A. WILLIAMSON *
JEAN K. DUDEK
RAYMOND R. MANDRA
LISA A. PIERONI
DOMINICK A. CONDE
STEVEN C. BAUMAN
ANNE M. MAHER
MARK J. ITRI *
BRIAN V. SLATER
DIEGO SCAMBIA
DANIEL CHUNG
TIMOTHY J. KELLY

DONNA MARIE WERNER
MICHAEL P. SANDONATO
WILLIAM C. HWANG
JOSEPH M. O'MALLEY, JR.
RONALD J. MCGAW
JOHN D. CARLIN
BRUCE M. WEXLER
JACK M. ARNOLD *
JOSEPH W. RAGUSA
WILLIAM J. ZAK, JR.
DANIEL S. GLUECK *
BRIAN L. KLOCK *
PAUL A. PYSHER *
DOLORES MORO-GROSSMAN
GREGORY B. SEPHTON
PETER J. KNUDSEN
PETER J. ARMENIO
DOUGLAS SHARROTT
THOMAS D. PEASE
ROBERT S. MAYER
T. THOMAS GELLENTHIEN *

ROBERT C. KLINE *
COUNSEL

* NOT ADMITTED IN NEW YORK

WASHINGTON OFFICE
1001 PENNSYLVANIA AVENUE, N.W.
WASHINGTON, D.C. 20004-2505
(202) 347-8100
FACSIMILE (202) 347-8136

CALIFORNIA OFFICE
650 TOWN CENTER DRIVE, SUITE 740
COSTA MESA, CALIFORNIA 92626-1925
(714) 540-8700
FACSIMILE (714) 540-9823

March 25, 1996

CERTIFIED MAIL
RETURN RECEIPT REQUESTED

Mr. Wilber Winkle
5764 Stevens Forest Rd. #606
Columbia, Maryland 21045

Re: Inquiry about Blue M&M's® chocolate candies

Dear Mr. Winkle:

We are trademark counsel for Mars, Incorporated and its M&M/Mars division. Your letter of December 13, 1995 addressed to Kathy Ljungquist has been referred to us.

The concept of launching a national campaign whereby consumers of M&M's® chocolate candies would vote for the addition of a new color to the existing color assortment originated with M&M/Mars' design agency prior to your letter of October 9, 1994 to Kathy Ljungquist. When the campaign was launched, the majority of the general public voted for the addition of the color blue over the colors pink and purple. As a result, the color blue was added to the assortment shortly thereafter.

Furthermore, M&M/Mars had previously used the color blue in its special color assortment for Independence Day which was introduced to the public during the 1986 holiday season.

We trust this resolves the matter.

Very truly yours,

FITZPATRICK, CELLA, HARPER & SCINTO

By:_____

Leslie K. Mitchell

April 6, 1996

Leslie K. Mitchell
Fitzpatrick, Cella, Harper & Scinto
277 Park Ave.
New York, NY 10172-0194

Dear Ms. Mitchell:

Thank you so much for taking the time to respond to my request for a thank-you note.
Now that's what I call customer service! To take time out of your busy schedule to
respond to a simple request for a thank-you note is going far beyond the call of duty.

And now, please allow me to make just a few comments about your letter. I was
disappointed not to receive a thank-you note for my idea. As you know, I first suggested
adding Blue M&Ms to Mars, Inc in a letter dated October 9, 1994. You claim the
decision was made before then, yet just seven months earlier Kathy Ljungquist denied
that any new colors were planned (see letter from Kathy enclosed).

I don't mean to make a big deal out of this, but it sure does look like you're trying to hide
something. Why else would Kathy give my letter to your law firm? Ms. Mitchell, I hope
you remember what happened in Watergate. If Nixon would have just admitted making a
mistake in the beginning, everything would have been fine. Instead, he chose to lie about
it, and then one lie turned into another and it ended up costing him his job. In a way, our
little ordeal is starting to look strangely familiar, isn't it?

And one other comment: You stated that the general public "voted" for the blue color.
As I've already stated to Ms. Ljungquist, the whole election was a farce. The fact that
"Blue" was challenged by such weak competitors as "Purple" and "Pink" is further
evidence that Mars, Inc. planned on adding "Blue" all along. As for your argument that
"Blue" already existed in a special display in 1986, I trust you realize that there's a
tremendous difference between adding a color for a gimmicky promotion and
permanently adding a color to the prestigious regular assortment, which I proposed in
October of 1994.

Ms. Mitchell, I kindly request once more that you send me a thank-you note for my idea.
But please don't send it certified this time. When the mailman knocked on the door last
time, I thought I'd won a sweepstakes or something. I look forward to hearing from you.

Very truly yours,

Wilber Winkle
5764 Stevens Forest Rd. #606
Columbia, MD 21045

FITZPATRICK, CELLA, HARPER & SCINTO
277 PARK AVENUE
NEW YORK 10172-0194
212-758-2400
FACSIMILE (212) 758-2982

JOSEPH M. FITZPATRICK
LAWRENCE F. SCINTO
WILLIAM J. BRUNET
ROBERT L. BAECHTOLD
JOHN A. O'BRIEN
JOHN A. KRAUSE
HENRY J. RENK
DAVID F. RYAN
PETER SAXON
ANTHONY M. ZUPCIC
CHARLES P. BAKER
STEVAN J. BOSSES
EDWARD E. VASSALLO
RONALD A. CLAYTON
NICHOLAS M. CANNELLA
HUGH C. BARRETT
DAVID M. QUINLAN
PASQUALE A. RAZZANO
JOHN W. BEHRINGER *
LAWRENCE A. STAHL

LEONARD P. DIANA
WILLIAM M. WANNISKY *
NINA SHREVE
ROBERT H. FISCHER
DONALD J. CURRY
WARREN E. OLSEN *
NICHOLAS N. KALLAS
BRUCE C. HAAS
ABIGAIL F. COUSINS
THOMAS H. BECK
LAWRENCE S. PERRY
MICHAEL K. O'NEILL
RICHARD P. BAUER *
ERROL B. TAYLOR
NICHOLAS GROOMBRIDGE
LESLIE K. MITCHELL
SCOTT K. REED
FREDRICK M. ZULLOW
SCOTT D. MALPEDE *
THOMAS J. O'CONNELL *

LAURA A. BAUER
CHRISTOPHER P. WRIST
GARY M. JACOBS *
STEVEN E. WARNER *
VICTOR J. GERACI
MARYANNE DICKEY
PENINA WOLLMAN
STEVEN C. KLINE
DAVID L. SCHAEFFER
JACK CUBERT *
MARK A. WILLIAMSON *
JEAN K. DUDEK
RAYMOND R. MANDRA
LISA A. PIERONI
DOMINICK A. CONDE
STEVEN C. BAUMAN
ANNE M. MAHER
MARK J. ITRI *
BRIAN V. SLATER
DIEGO SCAMBIA
DANIEL CHUNG
TIMOTHY J. KELLY

DONNA MARIE WERNER
MICHAEL P. SANDONATO
WILLIAM C. HWANG
JOSEPH M. O'MALLEY, JR.
RONALD J. MCGAW
JOHN D. CARLIN
BRUCE M. WEXLER
JACK M. ARNOLD *
JOSEPH W. RAGUSA
WILLIAM J. ZAK, JR.
DANIEL S. GLUECK *
BRIAN L. KLOCK *
PAUL A. PYSHER *
DOLORES MORO-GROSSMAN
GREGORY B. SEPHTON
PETER J. KNUDSEN
PETER J. ARMENIO
DOUGLAS SHARROTT
THOMAS D. PEASE
ROBERT S. MAYER
T. THOMAS GELLENTHIEN *

ROBERT C. KLINE *
COUNSEL

* NOT ADMITTED IN NEW YORK

WASHINGTON OFFICE
1001 PENNSYLVANIA AVENUE, N.W.
WASHINGTON, D.C. 20004-2505
(202) 347-8100
FACSIMILE (202) 347-8136

CALIFORNIA OFFICE
650 TOWN CENTER DRIVE, SUITE 740
COSTA MESA, CALIFORNIA 92626-1925
(714) 540-8700
FACSIMILE (714) 540-9823

April 16, 1996

CERTIFIED MAIL
RETURN RECEIPT REQUESTED

Mr. Wilber Winkle
5764 Stevens Forest Rd. #606
Columbia, Maryland 21045

      Re: Inquiry about Blue M&M's® chocolate candies

Dear Mr. Winkle:

We are in receipt of your letter of April 6, 1996.

As we stated in our previous letter, the concept of adding a new color to the existing color assortment originated with M&M/Mars' design agency prior to your letter of October 9, 1994 to Kathy Ljungquist.

As I am sure you can understand, M&M/Mars does not disclose information to the public about new products or concepts while in the development phase.

We trust this resolves the matter and will now close our file.

Very truly yours,

FITZPATRICK, CELLA, HARPER & SCINTO

By: _____
Leslie K. Mitchell

157

May 3, 1996

Leslie K. Mitchell, Attorney
Patrick, Cella, Harper & Scinto
277 Park Ave.
New York, NY 10172-0194

NO REPLY RECEIVED

Dear Ms. Mitchell

Thanks for your letter of April 16. I think it's pretty neat that you actually have a file there on me. I really never intended to cause all of this controversy, and this matter could have been resolved months ago if your client would have simply acknowledged that I was the brainstorm behind adding the Blue M&Ms to the color assortment. Now all my friends are telling me to sue you because you're not being up front with me. They say they could tell from the tone of your letters that you're trying to hide something, as why else would some big shot attorney like you become involved in such a trivial matter as this?

I'll tell you what we can do: I'll agree to settle the case for 5 one pound bags of M&Ms. Send me a release with the candy and I'll be happy to sign and return it. After all, it would probably be cheaper for you to settle the matter now than keep sending all those costly certified letters. I asked you in my last letter to stop sending them, but you did it anyway. My friends say that you are using that as a psychological weapon to wear me down. It's not going to work, Ms. Mitchell, so I would use the regular mail this time if I were you. I'm not you, of course, but I'm just saying that *if* I were, I would use the regular mail.

I hope to hear back soon about my proposed settlement.

Very truly yours,

Wilber Winkle
5764 Stevens Forest Rd. #606
Columbia, MD 21045

May 26, 1994

Mr. Pat Sajak
Wheel of Fortune
Studio Plaza
3400 Riverside Drive, 2nd Floor
Burbank, CA 91505

Dear Pat:

Congratulations on the pregnancy of your wife, Vanna. You make a cute couple and I'm pleased that you've finally decided to have some kids. If she's a baby girl, why not name her "Fortune"? I think Fortune Sajak has a nice ring to it.

I'd like to take this opportunity to ask you a few questions that have been on my mind for quite awhile:
1) Will Vanna take some time off after she's had the baby?
2) Any plans to raise the costs of vowels? At $250 a vowel, it's too easy to buy them all and then solve the puzzle. Let's put some skill back into the game!
3) The rickety sound of the wheel turning has become really annoying to me. Why not use a new computerized wheel with sound effects? That ought to boost the ratings!

Congratulations once again, Pat, from your biggest fan. Take care of Vanna. And I can't wait to hear back from you.

Very truly yours,

Wilber Winkle
5764 Stevens Forest Road #606
Columbia, MD 21045

WHEEL OF FORTUNE

June 7, 1994

Wilber Winkle
5764 Stevens Forest Road #606
Columbia, MD
21045

Dear Wilber,

Thank you for taking the time to write to Wheel of Fortune. We do appreciate hearing from our viewers.

Firstly, Pat and Vanna are not married. They never have been. Pat's been married to Lesly Brown for four years and Vanna's been married to George Santo Pietro for three. "Fortune" is a lovely name, but Vanna is due to have a boy. We are on summer hiatus now (as evidenced by the reruns airing currently) and Vanna doesn't come back to work until August. So she'll be right back on the new shows in September, never missing a beat.

We have no plans to raise the cost of vowels. And no plans to convert the wheel to a computer. Some viewers are wary of computers and feel they can be rigged, which of course will never happen on Wheel, but viewers don't want the change anyway.

Thanks again for your interest in our show. We hope you'll keep watching and enjoying Wheel of Fortune.

Best Regards,
Wheel of Fortune

Brian J. Palermo
Production Secretary

3400

Riverside

Drive

Burbank,

California

91505-4627

Tel:

818 972 793

Fax:

818 972 039

MERV GRIFFIN ENTERPRISES a SONY PICTURES ENTERTAINMENT company

July 9, 1993

Chrysler Corporation
P.O. Box 302
Centerline, MI 48015-9302

Dear Sirs:

I've been fascinated with automobile crash tests for years. I think it's super that your company is concerned enough with the safety of car owners and passengers that you conduct such testing. I bet Toyota & Mitsubishi don't test their cars as much as you guys do. Which is why I'm writing today. I have a suggestion to make your testing even better.

I would like to be the first human crash test victim. I figure that if those auto racers can roll their vehicles at 200 M.P.H. and still walk away without a scratch, then I can certainly crash one of your fine vehicles into a wall at 50 M.P.H. and survive. Unlike the dummies you use, I can then report back to you firsthand what parts of my body got hurt and suggest modifications to the vehicle that will correct any safety problems detected.

Aside from wanting to make your vehicles safer, I just lost my job at Burger King and I could really use the bucks. I figure $1,000 a test would be fair. With that kind of pay, I could do one test a week and make a half-decent living. Of course, I would also need medical insurance in case I get hurt real bad.

I'm very excited about my idea and I look forward to receiving your job application in the mail.

Very truly yours,

Wilber Winkle
5764 Stevens Forest Road #606
Columbia, MD 21045

CHRYSLER CORPORATION

Chrysler Corporation

07/29/93

Mr. Wilber Winkle
5764 Stevens Forest Rd. #606
Columbia, MD 21045

Dear Mr. Winkle:

Thank you for your letter of 7/9/93 in which you offered to become
our "first human crash test victim". We appreciate your taking the
time to contact our corporation.

While we appreciate your thinking of us as we work to improve the
safety of motor vehicle occupants, we nevertheless must refuse your
kind offer. The potential for injury in high speed test collisions
is great and we much prefer to conduct our tests with instrumented
crash dummies rather than risk a human life.

We're sure you will find another more suitable job very soon. We
trust it will be in some career field with better prospects for a
safe and secure future.

Thank you again for your interest in our test programs. At
Chrysler, we always enjoy hearing from our friends and customers.

Sincerely,

Charles R. Cheney
Outside Suggestions

SECTION THREE

I COULDN'T HELP MYSELF

October 11, 1993

United Airlines
Attention: <u>Consumer Relations</u>
P.O. Box 66100
Chicago, IL 60666

Dear Sirs:

I applaud your recent efforts enforcing weight restrictions on flight attendants. After all, you're in the business of flying planes, not blimps.

As a frequent air traveler, I look forward to having slim flight attendants greet me inside the plane with a warm smile. Not only do I have an eye for the ladies, but I also have a physical impairment – a bladder control problem that necessitates frequent trips to the lavatory (the coffee goes right through me). On a plane, there's nothing more annoying than trying to squeeze past some "cow" en route to the restroom. And, let me tell you, sometimes a few seconds can make all the difference in the world to me.

From what I understand, some of these "hippos" are suing you guys for imposing the weight restrictions. I just wanted to let you know that I'm available to testify on your behalf. Don't worry, I'm not ashamed to talk about my "problem" in court.

I look forward to hearing from you.

Very truly yours,

Wilber Winkle
5764 Stevens Forest Road #606
Columbia, MD 21045

March 23, 1994

United Airlines
<u>Attention</u>: Consumer Relations
P.O. Box 66100
Chicago, IL 60666

Dear Sirs:

Haven't seen or heard anything in the news lately about the lawsuit filed against you by
the overweight flight attendants. I assume it's still making its way through the court
system. Just wanted to let you know that I'm still willing and able to testify – before or
during the trial -- on the airline's behalf.

Enclosed, too, is a generous donation of $10.00 to help with legal expenses.

I look forward to hearing back from you soon.

Very truly yours,

Wilber Winkle
5764 Stevens Forest Road #606
Columbia, MD 21045

UNITED AIRLINES

Executive Offices

April 26, 1994

Mr. Wilbur Winkle
5764 Stevens Forest Road #606
Columbia, MD 21045

Dear Mr. Winkle:

Thank you for your courtesy in writing to comment about our weight policy and offer your testimony in court.

By way of background, height/weight guidelines for flight attendants were voluntarily agreed to by United's flight attendant union, the Association of Flight Attendants, as a result of a settlement of Federal court litigation which upheld the company's right to impose weight standards, but found that the standards being utilized were discriminatory toward women. Height/weight guidelines such as those contained in United's appearance program have been approved as lawful by the U.S. Supreme Court and numerous Federal courts.

In current negotiations between United and the Association, both parties have proposed to eliminate the weight program; overall appearance standards for flight attendants are still an issue. We are hopeful that these issues can be resolved through negotiation and not through the court system. With thanks for your concern, we are therefore returning your donation of a Travelers Express Company money order in the amount of $10.00 enclosed with your recent letter.

Again, thank you for interest in United Airlines as well as your support as a loyal customer.

Sincerely,

Sara Fields
Vice President
Inflight Service

Encl.

cc: P. R. Tinebra
     M. J. Gutsmiedl

P.O. Box 66100, Chicago, Illinois 60666 • Location: Elk Grove Township, Illinois, on Route 62, one-half mile west of Route 83

August 19, 1996

Consumer Relations Dept.
L'eggs Products
P.O. Box 450
Winston Salem, NC 27102

Dear Sirs:

Your *L'eggs* pantyhose are fantastic!!! I've been having a great time with them and wanted to take a moment to express my appreciation for a fine product. I recently discovered that when I slide your pantyhose over my face, it distorts my features and makes me look positively grotesque. Don't ask me why I did this in the first place, but let's just say things have been somewhat slow around here recently.

My favorite ploy is to take the elevator down to the lobby, where there's usually a small crowd gathered waiting to get on. When the doors open, I dramatically jump out and unleash a Tarzan-like scream. The reactions I get are priceless. One lady's knees buckled upon seeing me and she actually had to grab a railing for support. Another guy spilled his coffee all over his shirt. It was hilarious, yet I guess you had to be there to fully appreciate the magic of the moment.

Unfortunately, some spoil-sport actually complained to Management about my escapades, and now they've told me to knock them off. It seems *some* people just don't have a sense of humor anymore. I guess I'm going to have to take my act on the road now, and I'm anxious to see how it will play at malls, restaurants, movie theaters, etc.

Since it's obvious I'll garner a lot of attention, you may want to forward this letter to your marketing folks. They may want to capitalize on all the publicity I'll undoubtedly receive. Sure, I've tried other brands, but none can match the horrific facial distortions I receive from *L'eggs* pantyhose. To me, it sounds like a whole new market you may want to tap into. I look forward to hearing back from you on how we should proceed.

Thanks again for your wonderful product. Your pantyhose have made this a summer to remember.

Very truly yours,

Wilber Winkle

Wilber Winkle
5764 Stevens Forest Rd. #606
Columbia, MD 21045

L'eggs Products

Division of Sara Lee Corporation
Post Office Box 450
Winston-Salem, NC 27102

August 23, 1996

Mr. Wilber Winkle
5764 Stevens Forest Rd
#606
Columbia, MD 21045

Dear Mr. Winkle:

Thank you for your recent letter.

I have shared your letter with our Marketing Department and we feel at this time this is not the direction we want to pursue with our hosiery.

Thank you for your interest in our product.

Sincerely,

Carolyn Brown
Consumer Services Representative
Consumer Services

221050/0001

May 14, 1996

Delta Airlines
Attn: Ronald W. Allen, CEO
Hartsfield Atlanta International Airport
Atlanta, GA 30320

Dear Mr. Allen:

I've noticed that the barf bags on your planes don't have a manufacturer's name on them. Is the maker ashamed of them? Well, they shouldn't be. In my humble opinion, the barf bags on your planes are the best! Please supply me the name of the company that makes them so I can order a few on my own.

You may be wondering, what on earth would I want with a bunch of barf bags? Well, let's just say I've discovered a great new hobby.

A few minutes into each flight, I grab the airline-supplied barf bag and set it on my tray table in front of me. Generally, this attracts a quick glance or two in my direction, but nothing dramatic. A few minutes later, I open the bag and firmly clutch it in my right hand. This stage of the process usually results in a lot of fidgeting by the people seated around me. Then, after holding the bag tightly for a few minutes, I begin to moan and, with my left hand, gently massage my belly. At this point, all hell breaks loose! One guy on a recent flight actually leaped out of his seat and into the aisle! Interestingly, I've never made it beyond this point, as usually I burst out laughing myself, but the reactions I get are absolutely wonderful!

In fact, I enjoy this new hobby so much that I want to try it in other settings as well, such as ballgames, restaurants, elevators, etc. I therefore need a supply of the bags, and would like to order from the same company that makes Delta's.

I look forward to hearing back from you.

Very truly yours,

Wilber Winkle
5764 Stevens Forest Rd. #606
Columbia, MD 21045

Delta Air Lines, Inc.
Post Office Box 20980
Atlanta, Georgia 30320-2980

June 11, 1996

Mr. Wilber Winkle
5764 Stevens Forest Road, #606
Columbia, Maryland 21045

Dear Mr. Winkle:

Thank you for your recent correspondence to Mr. Allen regarding your interest in purchasing our air sickness bags. If this particular product is made available to the public in the retail market by the vendor, a representative will contact you.

We will always welcome the opportunity to be of service whenever your plans call for air travel.

Sincerely,

C. L. Myers
Senior Coordinator
Consumer Affairs

CLM:cmx

July 1, 1996

J.L. Reichert, CEO
Brunswick Corp.
1 N. Field Ct.
Lake Forest, IL 60045-4811

Dear Mr. Reichert:

I would like to place an order for a humongous, custom-made bowling ball. It should be about 8 feet high, and if my calculations are correct, weigh approximately 7,000 pounds. I'm willing to spend up to $10,000 for it, so money is definitely not a problem. Nor is shipping. As soon as the ball is ready, let me know and I'll rent a U-haul to pick it up.

As for the finger holes, please make them large enough for my entire arms to fit in them. This will allow me to get some decent velocity on the ball.

I don't want to bore you with all my detailed, ball-related plans, but let's just say they involve my girlfriend's mother. Lately, she's really been hassling me about everything. Boy, is she going to be in for a big surprise!

Please send me an order form or whatever paperwork you require. In the meantime, just to get things moving, I've enclosed a down payment of $10.

Thanks for your help!

Very truly yours,

Wilber Winkle
5764 Stevens Forest Rd. #606
Columbia, MD 21045

BRUNSWICK BOWLING   525 WEST LAKETON AVENUE   POST OFFICE BOX 329   MUSKEGON, MI 49443-0329   616-725-3300

July 10, 1996

Mr. Wilber Winkle
5764 Stevens Forest Road #606
Columbia, MD   21045

Dear Mr. Winkle:

Your letter of July 1, 1996 addressed to J. L. Reichert has been referred to our office for response. Your order for an 8 foot high, 7,000 pound bowling ball is a "first" for our division; unfortunately, Brunswick cannot comply with your request. We do not have the capability, nor the room, to manufacture a bowling ball of this size.

Please find enclosed your Money Order in the amount of $10. Mr. Winkle, hopefully things are going better with your mother-in-law and you have resolved your problems. If not, maybe you can treat her to lunch with the $10. Best regards.

Sincerely,

BRUNSWICK CORPORATION

Colette A. Heneveld
Administrative Assistant
Brunswick Indoor Recreation Group

Enclosure

December 16, 1995

L.R. Raymond, CEO
Exxon
225 East John W. Carpenter Freeway
Irving, TX 75062-2298

Dear Mr. Raymond:

Merry Christmas!!!   Wanted to drop you a note letting you know how much I enjoy the smell of your gas. Just so the aroma stays with me throughout the day, I purposely spill some gas on my hands in the morning, whenever I fill up the tank. My friends say I'm a jackass for doing this, but that doesn't stop me.

Is there anything wrong with sprinkling a little gas on your hands? I'm not a smoker, so it's not like I'm gonna blow up or anything.

Very truly yours,

Wilber Winkle
5764 Stevens Forest Rd. #606
Columbia, MD 21045

P.S. I note that you're based in Irving, Texas, home of the Dallas Cowboys. Boy, that coach Barry Switzer sure is an idiot. Can you believe that last week, in a tie game, he went for it on 4th and 1 from his own 29?! Frankly, I think the man should be fired for such a call. I also think the Cowboys will make it to the Conference Final against the 49ers, but they don't have a chance of beating San Francisco. My prediction:

49ers   *34*
Cowboys   *13*

EXXON COMPANY, U.S.A.

P.O. BOX 2180 - HOUSTON, TEXAS 77252 - 2180

MARKETING DEPARTMENT
FUEL PRODUCTS

DAVID E. ALLAN
BUSINESS SERVICES
STAFF ADVISOR

January 5, 1996

Mr. Wilber Winkle
5764 Stevens Forest Road, #606
Columbia, MD 21045

Dear Mr. Winkle:

Recently you wrote to our Corporate Headquarters in Irving about your preference for the odor of our gasoline.

Although we are very proud of our fuel quality, it is intended for use in motor vehicles rather than on the skin or for its odor properties. There are many reasons why the practice of deliberately using gasoline on the skin is not appropriate or wise. We would advise you to discontinue this practice.

We appreciate your interest and hope you continue to use Exxon gasoline in your vehicles. Please let us know if we can be of further assistance.

Very truly yours,

David E. Allan

December 30, 1995

Ritz Crackers
Nabisco Foods
<u>Attention</u>: Customer Service Dpt.
East Hanover, NJ 07936

Dear Sirs:

I live on the sixth floor of an apartment building and, from my balcony, like to throw Ritz Crackers at people on the ground below. I've briefly scared a few people, but they usually laugh as soon as they realize it's only a cracker that's falling on or near them.

Just thought you'd like to know how much pleasure your crackers give me and so many others.

Very truly yours,

Wilber Winkle
5764 Stevens Forest Rd. #606
Columbia, MD 21045

100 DeForest Avenue
P.O. Box 1911
East Hanover, NJ 07936-1911
1-800-NABISCO

January 17, 1996

Mr. Wilber Winkle
5764 Stevens Forest Road
#606
Columbia MD 21045

Dear Mr. Winkle:

Thank you for contacting Nabisco.

We appreciate your taking the time to express your views about your
usage of Ritz Crackers. We welcome your comments and will be sure to
share them with the appropriate people in our company.

Again, thanks for bringing this matter to our attention and for
being a Nabisco consumer.

Sincerely,

Phyllis Short
Consumer Representative
Consumer Information Services

April 5, 1996

Phyllis Short, Consumer Representative
Nabisco Foods Group
100 Deforest Ave.
P.O. Box 1911
East Hanover, NJ 07936-1911

Dear Ms. Short:

I was relieved to hear that your company supports me in my hobby of throwing Ritz Crackers at people from my sixth floor balcony. I kinda thought you would, as I'm sure you appreciate the free publicity I give your crackers.

Tossing them from my apartment really has been fun. Sometimes I duck after throwing them, and it's amusing to see my targets looking up and around, wondering how Ritz crackers could be falling from the sky. I can only do this for an hour or so at a stretch because my ribs usually start aching from so much laughing.

Bad news, Ms. Short. I'm afraid I'm going to have to cut out my cracker-throwing habit. My neighbors are no longer laughing when I hit them with the crackers, and some have even complained to Management. The Manager told me my practice was a nuisance to the other residents and that I should "cease immediately."

I've now thought of a good way of making amends to all my neighbors. Here's my plan. There are 179 residents in my building. I'm going to buy one box of Ritz crackers for each resident, leave it outside their apartment's front door, and attach a note telling them to bring their boxes to the volleyball court at 2:00 P.M. on a certain day. Then, when all the neighbors gather, I'm going to blow a whistle and tell everybody to rip open their boxes and start throwing the crackers at one another. Can you imagine how hilarious it'll be to watch 179 people throwing crackers at each other? I can't stop laughing just thinking about it.

Ms. Short, I have just one small problem. At normal retail prices, 179 boxes of Ritz Crackers will cost me over $500. I was just wondering: Could I buy the boxes in bulk in order to get a discounted rate? I figure I can spend about $300 all told, so if I have to buy at regular retail, I'll be able to buy boxes for only half of the neighbors. That, I'm sure you'd agree, just wouldn't be fair. I've enclosed a money order in the amount of $10 to get the ball rolling. Please let me know what I must do to receive the full cracker shipment. .

Very truly yours

Wilber Winkle
5764 Stevens Forest Rd. #606
Columbia, MD 21045

April 23, 1996

Mr. Wilber Winkle
5764 Stevens Forest Road
#606
Columbia MD 21045

Dear Mr. Winkle:

Thank you for contacting Nabisco.

We are sorry that we are unable to accomodate your request for 500
boxes of Ritz Crackers. We do not have products at this office nor
can we accept checks or money orders from our consumers.

Enclosed is your money order for $10.

Sincerely,

Phyllis Short
Consumer Representative
Consumer Information Services

May 18, 1996

Phyllis Short
Nabisco
100 Deforest Ave.
P.O. Box 1911
East Hanover, NJ 07936-1911

Dear Ms. Short:

I'm appalled at how you responded April 23 to my inquiry about buying large quantities of Ritz crackers. It's quite obvious that you gave my letter only a cursory glance; I wanted to buy *179* boxes of crackers, not 500 as you said in your letter. Why would I want 500 boxes of crackers? I've already told you there are only 179 people in my building. What on earth would I or they do with an extra 321 boxes of crackers?

What's most annoying is that you didn't even extend me the common courtesy of telling me where I can meet my cracker-supply needs. Is that any way to treat a customer who's going to buy hundreds of dollars worth of crackers? It appears to me that you're just trying to swat me away like an irritating insect. Frankly, Ms. Short, I think you should do some serious soul searching to determine if you really have what it takes to be a Consumer Representative. Perhaps another line of work would be more suitable.

Let's give it one more shot: Please find enclosed a check for $10. If you can't process my order there at your offices, *please* forward my request to someone in your company who can. I think an apology is also in order, and I will await one with much anticipation.

Very truly yours,

Wilber Winkle

Wilber Winkle
5764 Stevens Forest Rd. #606
Columbia, MD 21045

P.S. Sorry if my letter sounded a bit harsh, but I guess I'm so anxious to start the "Cracker Battle" that I'm getting frustrated by the delays we seem to be encountering. No hard feelings, OK?

100 DeForest Avenue
P.O. Box 1911
East Hanover, NJ 07936-1911
1-800-NABISCO

May 28, 1996

Mr. Wilber Winkle
5764 Stevens Forest Road
#606
Columbia MD 21045

Dear Mr. Winkle:

Thank you for contacting Nabisco again.

Unfortunately, we are not able to fulfill your request or process
your check. We do not have the ability to provide our products to
our consumers at discount prices. We do recommend that you purchase
our crackers at any of your local supermarkets. In addition, we do
not condone the activities for which you intend to use our crackers.
We apologize for any misunderstanding. Enclosed, you will find your
money order which we are returning to you.

Again, thank you for your time and contacting us.

Sincerely,

Amanda L. Fossett, R.D.
Team Leader
Consumer Information Services

July 1, 1993

Harry Wendelstedt, Jr., National League Umpire
Harry Wendelstedt School for Umpires
88 South St. Andrews Drive
Ormond Beach, FL 32174

Dear Wendelstedt:

I have a dream. I'd like to be the first blind umpire in major league history. I guess the best place to start on this history-making journey would be your Umpire School, which is why I'm writing.

Although I lost my sight several years ago in a freak accident, I do believe I'll make an excellent umpire. As I'm sure you know, blind people hear much better than normal people. That's the secret to my success. I'm able to call balls and strikes by listening to where the ball hits the catcher's mitt. Also, when the batter swings, I can feel the slight breeze generated by the bat cutting through the air. If I feel a breeze and then hear the thump of the catcher's mitt, I know it's a swinging strike.

I must admit I do have some problems calling close plays around the bases. But I figure since there are four umps in every major league game, the other guys will be there to help me out. I've already umpired a girl's little league game and had only one argument with one of the managers. Everyone but him said I did a great job of umpiring.

So please enroll me in your school, Harry. I look forward to receiving your confirmation letter. And money's not a problem, as I get a bunch of checks from the government every month.

Very truly yours,

Wilber Winkle
5764 Stevens Forest Road #606
Columbia, MD 21045

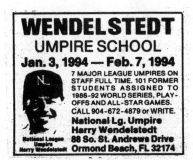

August 25, 1993

Harry Wendelstedt
National League Umpire
88 South St. Andrews Drive
Ormond Beach, FL 32174

Dear Mr. Wendelstedt:

Hi, Harry! Still haven't heard back from you with regard to my enrollment in the school. Please forgive me if our letters cross in the mail. I don't mean to be impatient, but I guess I am. January is only four months away and I'd like to purchase my airline tickets as soon as possible. It's much cheaper if you buy in advance.

Since writing last, I've gotten a few more games under my belt and my confidence is growing. Everyone marvels at my ability and predicts a great future for me in umpiring. Sure, I've missed a few calls, but everybody makes mistakes and none of mine affected the outcome of a game.

More good news! Remember my telling you about the argument I had with one of the girls' league managers? Well, the League Commissioner stepped in and said I won't have to umpire any more games involving his team.

Enclosed is a money order for my deposit.

Very truly yours,

Wilber Winkle
5764 Stevens Forest Road #606
Columbia, MD 21045

HARRY WENDELSTEDT
SCHOOL FOR UMPIRES
AT THE

Daytona Beach Resort Area

88 S. ST. ANDREWS DRIVE
ORMOND BEACH, FLORIDA 32174

Harry Wendelstedt, Jr., Pres.
Phone 904/672-4879

SEPT 29, 1993

DEAR MR. WINKLER,

I'M RETURNING YOUR CHECK (10.00).
IT WOULD BE IMPOSSIBLE FOR YOU TO
MAKE IT INTO PRO-BASEBALL. YOU WOULD
BE COMPETING AGAINST PEOPLE WITH
PERFECT VISION. 95% OF THOSE DON'T
MAKE IT. THIS PROFFESSION IS STRICTLY
SURVIVAL OF THE FITTEST. YOUR
DREAM IS IMPOSSIBLE.

I'M VERY SORRY TO RUIN YOUR
DREAM. SOMEBODY HAS TO BE HONEST
WITH YOU. I WISH YOU EVERY
SUCCESS IN FUTURE ENDEAVORS

SINCERELY
Harry Wendelstedt

6302 Stevens Forest Road
Columbia, MD 21045

November 13, 1993

Harry Wendelstedt
88 South St. Andrews Drive
Ormond Beach, FL 32174

Dear Mr. Wendelstedt,

Thanks so much for rejecting Wilber Winkle's application to your umpiring school. Your words must have really hit home because Wilber now realizes he doesn't have a bright future in umpiring.

I was a team manager in a league game where Wilber was umpiring and I can honestly say he was the worst ump I've ever seen. Things became so heated between Wilber and myself that the League Commissioner took him off all games involving my team. During the one game when he called balls and strikes, Wilber called one of my batters out even before the pitch was thrown, claiming he felt a breeze from the bat swinging and missing. I tried to tell him that the breeze he felt wasn't from the bat, but from a rapidly approaching storm, but he just wouldn't listen.

Now don't get me wrong. I'm all for helping the disabled in any way I can, but having Wilber umpire was taking things a bit too far. I will say this, though: Wilber made me realize how important a good umpire really is. And I know I can do better than those bums did in the World Series. Did you see how they kept calling those outside pitches strikes? The camera overtop home plate exposed those umpires for what they really are – a bunch of overpaid, overweight egomaniacs.

Please enroll me in your school, Mr. Wendelstedt. Enclosed is my application fee of $25.

Sincerely,

Peter Gabriel

HARRY WENDELSTEDT SCHOOL FOR UMPIRES

AT THE

Daytona Beach Resort Area

88 S. ST. ANDREWS DRIVE
ORMOND BEACH, FLORIDA 32174

Harry Wendelstedt, Jr., Pres.
Phone 904/672-4879

12/13/93

Dear Mr. Gabriel,
Enclosed please find your check for $25.00. If you desire to enroll, complete application and send proper deposit by return mail. The school opens in 3 weeks.

Thank you for your letter concerning the blind umpire. It would be impossible for him to qualify, I feel someone was pulling a cruel joke on the young man. You need excellent vision in this job.

Happy Holidays!

Harry Wendelstedt

THE WORLD'S MOST FAMOUS UMPIRE SCHOOL

SECTION FOUR

A LOT OF EXTRA STUFF

THE WRITING OF THIS BOOK

Dear Reader:

When a friend recently took an interest in my stress-relieving/problem-solving technique of complaint-writing and referred me to a book publisher, I was quite flattered. I was even more flattered when that publisher — Bruce Bortz of Bancroft Press — asked me to lunch. He said he'd reviewed the letters I had accumulated over the previous three years, and considered a few of them to be "hilarious," including the one to Chrysler where I'd requested a job as a human crash test dummy.

At first, I was puzzled by this comment. Then I became angry and confused. What, I demanded to know, did he mean by hilarious? "Well," came his nervous reply, "your letters are supposed to be funny, aren't they?"

In my younger days, I would have challenged Mr. Bortz to a brawl, laughed out of context, or picketed the Bancroft Press townhouse to protest the mocking of my efforts. Instead, I raced home to my computer and composed a complaint letter.

Mr. Bortz soon called to apologize for the "terrible mistake" he had made. My manuscript, he said, "had gotten mixed up with one he was looking over on presidential joke writers." But I was unsatisfied with this explanation. I asked him point blank: if he had truly made a "mistake," why had he specifically called my Chrysler letter hilarious? After a long pause, Mr. Bortz explained: "I thought you were proposing to do the crash tests without a seat belt."

"Only a fool would do a crash test that way," I responded, after which we both enjoyed a healthy chuckle. Mr. Bortz promptly proclaimed that the world would be a better place if all my letters were published, and that he wanted to do so in a Bancroft Press book. How could I not agree?

But the road ahead would still be a little bumpy. Over the next three months, we exchanged about a dozen letters, and finally agreed to the terms of a basic contract. After that, we began a long series of negotiations — mostly by e-mail — about the book's contents. Sometimes it was hard to agree. He'd want a letter in, and I wouldn't. He'd want a letter put in a certain place. I'd want it elsewhere. He said my face shouldn't be on the cover. I politely objected.

I suppose I wore him down because, six months later, our dickering finally ended and Mr. Bortz, sounding quite exasperated, wrote me to say, "I give up, Wilber. I'll put in whatever letters you want in whatever order you say and do whatever kind of cover you think best." I guess that means that, if you don't like any aspect of this book, you'd better complain directly to me, not to Mr. Bortz's Bancroft Press.

Except for one thing. In light of the lengthy back-and-forth I had with Mr. Bortz, you may think it strange that the book is located in the humor section of your library or bookstore. I do, too. I thought it should go on the "Self-Help" shelves, or maybe those of "Spirituality," "New Age," or "Inspiration." I insisted to Mr. Bortz that I'd written my letters, first and foremost, to help people like me — the ones who are always taken advantage of.

But, for once, he put his foot down. He maintained that shelving the book in "Humor" was "a good idea" because, as he put it, most people who browse in the humor section "lead miserable lives, and are desperately searching for something to enhance their stress-filled existences. These book buyers and book readers," Mr. Bortz concluded, "are the ones who will benefit the most from your wisdom, Wilber."

I could have objected to his reasoning and his shelving recommendation — after all, by then I'd complained about everything else related to the book. But, for once in my life, I was at the receiving end of some flattery, and so, against my better judgment, I let the shelving decision slide.

Let me explain, though, why I organized "Wilber Winkle Has A Complaint" the way I did. I put my out-and-out complaints in the first section. As you know by now, I often see the absurdity of our commercial world, and when it looks like its craziness will go uncountered, I'm the first to complain. Please note that whenever I talked "boycott" in these letters, I could always count on a direct response. The mere suggestion of "boycott" got under every CSR's skin.

But, as you've also seen from my letters, I've not been reluctant to serve up compliments, offer suggestions on how to improve products or product marketing, or seek valuable clarification about consumer goods and companies. I never got much in the way of thanks from the companies I wrote this kind of letter to, and sometimes, believe it or not, I ended up getting certified letters from their lawyers. But so be it. The letters where I tried to be a constructive critic are in the book's second section.

In the third section, I put the letters where my mischievous, even pranksterish side surfaced. For instance, I never really intended to roll a gigantic bowling ball over my girlfriend's mother. But I must admit that just the fantasy of doing so helped me get through some of her nagging barrages.

Unfortunately, if you knew nothing more about me than what's in this last batch of letters, you might think I'm interested only in creating havoc in other people's lives. In fact, these particular letters represent my own special way of peacefully releasing excessive tension and frustration. And though I remain ashamed of having lost control, of having gone a bit too far, on these occasions, I'm pleased to say they were isolated, and there was no need, throughout those numerous days of book preparation, to stray from my recommendation to Mr. Bortz that the title of this book be "Wilber Winkle Has A Complaint," and not "Wilber Winkle Goes Overboard."

Putting this book together hasn't been easy for me (or for Mr. Bortz), but it definitely has changed my life for the better. This is no longer a one-man crusade for me. I've gained a greater sense of responsibility to my fellow consumers. So, even if this book sells a million copies, I promise to go right on complaining "the Wilber Winkle way." I've finally found my life's calling.

Very truly yours,

Wilber Winkle

Wilber Winkle

189

COMPLAINING
THE WILBER WINKLE™ WAY

Dear Reader:

I'm certain you're convinced by now of all the benefits produced by my various letter writing campaigns. Aside from improving my own well-being, I've attacked dozens of consumer injustices and assisted millions who lacked the fortitude or resolve to do something for themselves. Lying in bed at night, I take comfort knowing that if my letters stop just one rogue waitress from re-filling a coffee mug that is still half-full, then the battle has been well worth it.

But I bet you're saying to yourself, "Sure, Wilber, you've had amazing success in your letter writing campaigns, but can I really make a difference, too?" While I can't promise you'll be as influential in world events as I have been, I can say with assurance that you will get results if you carefully follow my "17 Tips on Complaining the Wilber Winkle Way" below.

First, though, you must study these guidelines. In fact, you shouldn't even begin until you can recite each one in proper order. Friends have told me it helps to record them on tape and then play them back in the car when driving. Don't ever underestimate the importance of these tips, as customer service representatives are a savvy lot who will pounce on you like a tiger if they smell inexperience or lack of knowledge.

1. **USE ONLY WHITE STATIONERY.** Colored stationery often looks a little too cute, and letters written on them are likely to be dismissed as whimsical and lacking substance.

2. **USE 12 POINT FONT ON ALL LETTERS.** Ten point fonts give an impression of weakness and uncertainty, while 14 point fonts make you look dimwitted, as if you needed big letters to comprehend things.

3. **ADDRESS YOUR INITIAL COMPLAINTS TO THE TOP BANANA OF EACH CORPORATION,** not an underling. Sure, your letter will probably be passed down to the customer service representative (CSR) anyway, but at least you'll get a decent response, as most CSRs are all too anxious to show their bosses how effective they are in getting rid of you.

4. **DON'T HESITATE TO SHOW ON YOUR LETTERS THAT YOU'RE CARBON COPYING PROMINENT POLITICAL FIGURES** — like the president of the United States. This is especially effective when writing other elected officials. But save your stamps and don't actually send out the carbon copies; the very thought that the president is plugged into your grievance should ensure a proper response by the politico handling your letter.

5. **SEND MONEY** to get the CSRs stirring if you really feel passionate about your complaint. Sadly, many corporations cater to fat-cats these days, and tossing a little money their way will make you look more important and worthy of their time.

6. **STICK WITH GOOD, OLD-FASHIONED MAIL TO REGISTER YOUR COMPLAINTS.** I know this is the age of fax machines, modems, and voice-mail. But from lots of experience, I've found that it's much harder to phone in your complaints. Most companies have installed automated phone menus for the express purpose of getting us to hang up and leave them alone. In fact, studies they've done show that maneuvering through their voice-mail options is likely to increase the average consumer's stress levels by over 50%. Steer clear of voice mail!

7. **TIME YOUR MAILINGS SO LETTERS WILL ARRIVE AT THEIR DESTINATIONS ON THURSDAY.** At most places of business, Monday is "meeting day," when new techniques and strategies aimed at making consumers go away are discussed and analyzed in grueling day-long seminars. Tuesday is rushed — from trying to catch up on all the complaints received, but not acted upon, on Monday. On Wednesday, CSRs are extremely tired from all that running around on Tuesday. And Friday is generally reserved for horse-play and baby showers. Thursday is the only day when your letter will get the attention it so richly deserves.

8. **DON'T FORGET YOUR MAIL CARRIER!!!** You'll need to build a rapport with him (or her) so your letters will get preferential treatment at the post office. Start slowly — with remarks about the weather (e.g., "Looks like rain!"), followed by more intimate discussions on topics ranging from the local baseball team's pennant chances to the health of the carrier's mother. (WARNING: Don't ever bring up your high volume of junk mail. Such comments make mail carriers feel as if they're merely carrying around a sack of garbage all day).

9. **USING REGULAR MAIL IS OK**, unless your attempts at bonding with the mail carrier backfire and you come to blows with him (or her). If this occurs, and you therefore must eliminate the possibility of the mail carrier sabotaging your efforts, I suggest UPS or FedEx or any of the other private services. But remember: If you get into complaining in a big way, you'll get lots of personal mail every day, and a mail carrier with a grudge against you could destroy your cause.

10. **USE CERTIFIED MAIL** only when your letter is of such importance that failure to receive a prompt response could jeopardize the health of you and your family.

11. **ALLOW 30 DAYS FOR A RESPONSE TO YOUR COMPLAINT/INQUIRY.** If CSRs haven't responded by then, they are likely employing what's known in customer service circles as "The Silent Treatment," whereby they simply ignore your letter in the hopes that you will leave them alone. Sadly, this technique is very effective on the weak and down-trodden who aren't able to muster the energy to continue the fight.

12. **GET THE CSRs' ATTENTION IF THE 30 DAYS LAPSE** and a follow-up letter is necessary, by using "Lottery Headquarters" as your return address. That'll make them think they won something.

13. **RETURN ALL THE COUPONS CSRs UNDOUBTEDLY WILL SEND YOU.** Most coupons are secretly coded, and CSRs are notified whenever they're redeemed. If you use the coupons sent you, you will forever be labeled a "coupon caper," and as such you'll rarely get a fair shake with the issues you raise; CSRs know they can dismiss "capers" by merely sending them more coupons.

14. **BE PREPARED FOR FRUSTRATIONS.** As you can tell from reading my published correspondence, I often poured my heart and soul out to company executives, and sometimes got nothing but inappropriate form letters in return. But I didn't let that stop me. Naive I may be about a lot of things, but I also have a temper when I'm being jerked around. Corporate and Political America know when they've "done me wrong." You should do no less!

15. **SEND A SIMPLE "THANK YOU" TO CSRs** if they send you specific responses to your letters. You may even consider inviting them over for coffee if they are local. Building good relationships with CSRs is very important.

16. **ALWAYS PAY ATTENTION TO THE THINGS THAT ANNOY YOU.** Then pull out pen and paper, or turn your computer on, and give the people bringing stress to your life a piece of your mind — immediately. Believe me, it works a lot better than everything else I've tried, especially "rope-a-dope" and verbal fatalism.

17. **BE PERSISTENT.** Writing letters of complaint is the best way to correct the problems you experience with products and services, but you'll often have to correspond more than once to get a satisfactory response. CSRs respect consumers who show commitment to their cause, and what better way to demonstrate that than repeated mailings to the same individual?

Follow all my tips, and get ready to sleep better at night. Like me, you'll no longer be tormented by the riddles and ravages of everyday consumer life.

And get ready, too, to brag a little about your successes. I frequently dispense pearls of wisdom during conversational lulls on the cocktail circuit, where my unparalleled information base has made me the proverbial hit of the party. Fellow party-goers are in such awe of my knowledge that they often ask me, "Are you for real, Wilber?"

So get into the letter-writing spirit and head with me to the consumer barricades. We may not be able to change the world. But we can stand up to the companies that take away our favorite candy bar's almonds.

Very truly yours,

Wilber Winkle

CUSTOMER SERVICE LINGO

To successfully navigate your way through the world of consumer correspondence, you've got to learn the language. All customer service representatives (CSRs) endure a vigorous training program where they learn to tactfully dismiss your ideas and suggestions in order to meet their ultimate goal — getting rid of you. Once you've been in this game as long as I have, you'll start to pick up on the sly innuendoes and hidden meanings that often litter their responses. I thought it was only fair to save you some trouble interpreting CSR lingo and share with you what I've learned to date.

The following is a typical reply from an organization you've written to:

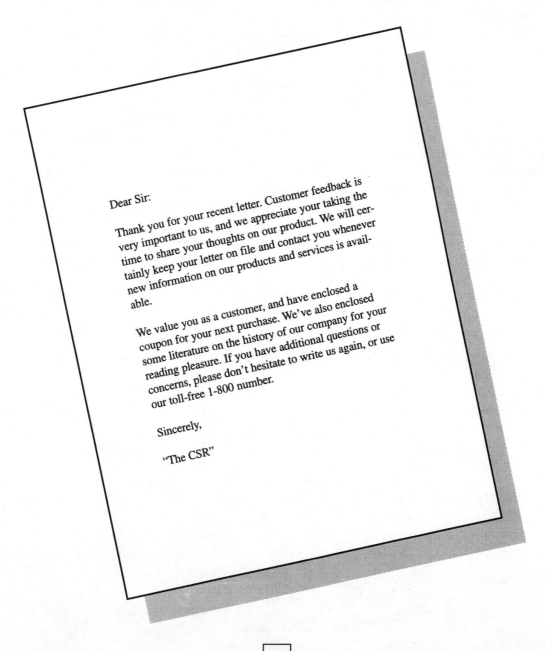

Dear Sir:

Thank you for your recent letter. Customer feedback is very important to us, and we appreciate your taking the time to share your thoughts on our product. We will certainly keep your letter on file and contact you whenever new information on our products and services is available.

We value you as a customer, and have enclosed a coupon for your next purchase. We've also enclosed some literature on the history of our company for your reading pleasure. If you have additional questions or concerns, please don't hesitate to write us again, or use our toll-free 1-800 number.

Sincerely,

"The CSR"

After receiving these letters for years, I'm now able to accurately interpret exactly what they mean.

When CSR's Write:	They Really Mean:
Thank you for your recent letter.	Thanks for the job security. If it wasn't for people like you, I wouldn't be on the payroll.
Customer feedback is very important to us.	They asked me to respond, even though I have no idea what you're writing about.
We will certainly keep your letter on file…	Your letter will be put in our shredder tomorrow.
… and contact you whenever new information on our products and services is available.	You'll never hear from us again.
We value you as a customer…	I'm sending you a letter which means nothing whatsoever.
… and have enclosed a coupon for your next purchase.	The coupon is enclosed because we figure that's the easiest way to get rid of you.
We've also enclosed some literature on our company for your reading pleasure.	If you find the enclosed literature interesting, then you need to get help.
If you have additional questions or concerns, please don't hesitate to write again…	Please think twice about writing us back…
… or use our toll-free 1-800 number.	Better yet, why not get tied up in our voice mail system?

Put it all together, and this is what they are really trying to tell you:

Dear Sir:

Thanks for the job security. If it wasn't for people like you, I wouldn't be on the payroll.

Because your letter, which will be put in our shredder tomorrow, is of such little interest to us, they asked me to respond, even though I have no idea what you're writing about.

To give you an idea of how much we value you, I'm sending you a letter which means nothing whatsoever. The coupon is enclosed merely because we figure that's the easiest way to get rid of you. If you find the enclosed literature about our company interesting, then you need to get help.

Please think twice before writing us back. Better yet, why not get tied up in our voice mail system?

Sincerely,

"The CSR"

MY WEB PAGE
www.wilberwinkle.com

Dear Reader:

Because I want to stay in touch with all of you, my readers, even after this book comes out, I decided to start my own web page. This page, I hope, will be a source of continuing inspiration and assistance to you. What I especially like about the webpage is that it allows true two-way communication.

Through the Wilber Winkle webpage, and its e-mail capability, you'll be able to:

- **TELL** me what products you'd like me to complain about on your behalf

- **SEND** along to me your nominations for favorite (and least favorite) letters from the book

- **MAKE** me your very own complaint consultant when you're having trouble writing complaint letters by yourself

- **GET** in touch with other aggrieved consumers

- **PLAY** complaint-simulation games and a lot, lot more.

On the Wilber Webpage, www.wilberwinkle.com, I'll also try to:

- **PUBLISH** for you some of the letters that couldn't fit in my book, the responses to letters that came in after the book was printed, and some of my letters that never got a response

- **TELL** you more about my life that there wasn't room for in the book

- **GIVE** you monthly updates on my activities, in connection with the book and otherwise — stuff like what shows I may be appearing on, what cities I may be visiting, and when and where I may be leading formal complaint-writing seminars

- **KEEP** you up to date on my newest targets of complaint — what I call "Wilber Winkle's Woeful Wonders"

- **BRING** to your attention the wiliest tactics of the best customer service representatives

- **PASS** along to you some of my best tips on how to write complaint letters — the ones that are treated with the seriousness they deserve

- **DETAIL** for you how you can join the Wilber Winkle Fan Club, and what perks you'll get if you become a member

- **GET** your comments on the book as a whole, and then pass them along to everybody else, and

- **LINK** you to other websites that relate to my book and to consumer complaints.

So check in regularly, and most of all remember: "Keep complaining the Wilber Winkle Way."

Very truly yours,

Wilber Winkle

Wilber Winkle

ABOUT THE AUTHOR

A resident of Maryland for most of his life, Wilber Winkle recently decided a change was in order after reviewing a petition signed by 172 of the 179 residents of his apartment community. Their desire to see Wilber head out onto the road and to expand his horizons was so strong that they actually packed and loaded all of his belongings for him. Wilber himself put it this way in a recent letter: "Many of the residents were so caught up in the emotion of my exodus that they were unable to gain the composure needed to bid me a proper farewell, and my persistent knocks on their doors went unanswered."

Driving for an entire day and much of the night, Wilber desperately searched for a sign that would tell him where to make his new home. He traveled more than 1,000 miles before finally spotting his beacon in the night. Pulling over to the shoulder of a deserted Interstate outside of Tampa, Florida, he stepped down from his truck, turned his nose to the air, and smelled the unmistakable aroma of Pepperidge Farm cookies. Four and a half miles later, a Pepperidge Farm Cookie Factory came into view.

"If you've ever tasted a Pepperidge Farm product," says Wilber, "I'm sure you can figure out why I settled here. A Pepperidge Farm cookie is as close to perfection as any product ever made. The factory's aroma will be a daily and constant reminder of how products can and should be manufactured and marketed."

Wilber's days in the Tampa area are filled with fairly everyday activities. He eats junk-food, goes to the mall, plays golf, rents videos, washes his clothes, and goes to the bank, all while keeping a very sharp eye out for products and services that do not meet his and our expectations. "My mission remains unfinished," says Wilber. "You can count on hearing much more from me in the months and years ahead."